BRANCH LINES TO ENFIELD TOWN AND PALACE GATES

Jim Connor

Series Editor Vic Mitchell

MP Middleton Press

Cover photograph : We look north from Seven Sisters Junction signal box and view class N7/5 0-6-2T No. 69663 departing from the station with the 1.16pm train from Enfield Town to Liverpool Street on 11th October 1958. The wooden platforms serving the Palace Gates branch can be seen to the left. (K.L. Cook / Rail Archive Stephenson)

ISBN 1 904474 32 2

First published June 2004

© *Middleton Press, 2004*

Published by
  Middleton Press
  Easebourne Lane
  Midhurst, West Sussex
  GU29 9AZ
Tel: 01730 813169
Fax: 01730 812601
Email : info@middletonpress.co.uk
www.middletonpress.co.uk

Layout and typesetting London Railway Record

Printed & bound by MPG Books Ltd, Bodmin, Cornwall.

INDEX

GEOGRAPHICAL SETTING

The lines are on the clays of the northern flank of the lower Thames Valley and were built through open farmland to a large extent. They were the prime cause for the urbanisation of the district in a short space of time. From a start at about 50ft above sea level, the tracks reach around the 100ft level at Enfield and 150ft at the gates at the foot of the hill on which the Alexandra Palace was constructed.

ACKNOWLEDGMENTS

I would like to thank all the photographers, without whose enthusiasm and interest in years gone by, albums such as this could not have been produced. I also wish to express my gratitude to Bryan Wilson of the SRS and GERS, who kindly supplied details of signal boxes, along with Ian Strugnell, whose assistance has been greatly appreciated.

In addition I must thank my good friend and regular *London Railway Record* contributor, Geoff Goslin, who provided an original *Railway Gazette* publication of 1920, from which much useful information was gleaned.

Finally, mention must be made of the various company and Board of Trade files which are held at the National Archives, Kew. These provide the researcher with a wealth of facts and are an essential asset to all who are involved in the study of railway history.

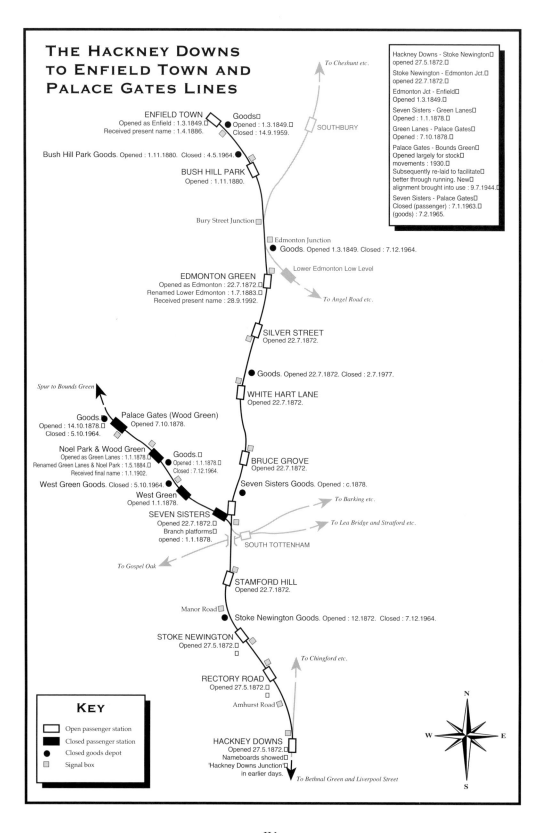

THE HACKNEY DOWNS TO ENFIELD TOWN AND PALACE GATES LINES

To Cheshunt etc.

Hackney Downs - Stoke Newington
opened 27.5.1872.
Stoke Newington - Edmonton Jct.
opened 22.7.1872.
Edmonton Jct - Enfield
Opened 1.3.1849.
Seven Sisters - Green Lanes
Opened : 1.1.1878.
Green Lanes - Palace Gates
Opened : 7.10.1878.
Palace Gates - Bounds Green
Opened largely for stock
movements : 1930.
Subsequently re-laid to facilitate
better through running. New
alignment brought into use : 9.7.1944.
Seven Sisters - Palace Gates
Closed (passenger) : 7.1.1963.
(goods) : 7.2.1965.

ENFIELD TOWN
Opened as Enfield : 1.3.1849.
Received present name : 1.4.1886.

Goods.
Opened : 1.3.1849.
Closed : 14.9.1959.

SOUTHBURY

Bush Hill Park Goods. Opened : 1.11.1880. Closed : 4.5.1964.

BUSH HILL PARK
Opened : 1.11.1880.

Bury Street Junction

Edmonton Junction
Goods. Opened 1.3.1849. Closed : 7.12.1964.

Lower Edmonton Low Level

EDMONTON GREEN
Opened as Edmonton : 22.7.1872.
Renamed Lower Edmonton : 1.7.1883.
Received present name : 28.9.1992.

To Angel Road etc.

SILVER STREET
Opened 22.7.1872.

Goods. Opened 22.7.1872. Closed : 2.7.1977.

WHITE HART LANE
Opened 22.7.1872.

Spur to Bounds Green

Goods.
Opened : 14.10.1878.
Closed : 5.10.1964.

Palace Gates (Wood Green)
Opened 7.10.1878.

Noel Park & Wood Green
Opened as Green Lanes : 1.1.1878.
Renamed Green Lanes & Noel Park : 1.5.1884.
Received final name : 1.1.1902.

Goods.
Opened : 1.1.1878.
Closed : 7.12.1964.

West Green Goods. Closed : 5.10.1964.

West Green
Opened 1.1.1878.

BRUCE GROVE
Opened 22.7.1872.

Seven Sisters Goods. Opened : c.1878.

To Barking etc.

To Lea Bridge and Stratford etc.

SEVEN SISTERS
Opened 22.7.1872.
Branch platforms
opened : 1.1.1878.

SOUTH TOTTENHAM

To Gospel Oak

STAMFORD HILL
Opened 22.7.1872.

Manor Road

Stoke Newington Goods. Opened : 12.1872. Closed : 7.12.1964.

STOKE NEWINGTON
Opened 27.5.1872.

To Chingford etc.

RECTORY ROAD
Opened 27.5.1872.

Amhurst Road

KEY

☐ Open passenger station
■ Closed passenger station
● Closed goods depot
▪ Signal box

HACKNEY DOWNS
Opened 27.5.1872.
Nameboards showed
'Hackney Downs Junction'
in earlier days.

To Bethnal Green and Liverpool Street

N
W   E
S

HISTORICAL BACKGROUND

THE ENFIELD LINE

Today's route linking Hackney Downs with Enfield Town dates from 1872, although the section north of Edmonton is much older.

Our story starts back in 1849, when the Eastern Counties Railway opened a branch from its existing Lea Valley Line to the Middlesex town of Enfield. This had been sanctioned by the Enfield & Edmonton Railway Bill of 1846 and its single track stretched for a distance of 3miles 7chains. The branch left the Lea Valley Line a little to the north of what is now Angel Road station and terminated close to the centre of Enfield where an existing house was adapted as the station building.

Because much of the route was still rural at the time there was little demand for the trains, but with the spread of suburbia during the following decades it became apparent that the area needed a more direct link with central London.

In 1862 the ECR became part of the larger Great Eastern Railway and the new organisation lost no time in pressing for improvements. On 29th July 1864, the GER (Metropolitan Station & Railways) Act was authorised by Parliament. This included the construction of a new line from Bethnal Green, which would be carried on viaduct towards Hackney Downs, then continue to Lower Edmonton where it would join the original route of 1849.

Unfortunately the company lacked the necessary finances at the time, so work on the section between Hackney Downs and Lower Edmonton did not start until the early part of 1870.

Around this time the GER was also busy building a new City terminus at Liverpool Street, as a replacement for its inconveniently sited premises at Bishopsgate which had been inherited from the Eastern Counties Railway. The construction of the station and its approach tracks resulted in the demolition of many existing buildings, including housing and the company was therefore obligated to assist those who had been displaced. The authorising Act of 1864 included a clause whereby the GER had to run at least one daily train in both directions between Lower Edmonton and London, on which special 2d workmen return tickets were

valid. With this facility available, the developers moved in and after a short while streets of new terraced houses began to spring up along the route, particularly around Edmonton, where, within less than a decade, the population rose by 70%.

The GER more than met its obligation by operating two 2d return trains from the outset, although at first services only stretched between Stoke Newington and Bishopsgate.

The line from Bethnal Green Junction to Stoke Newington opened to passenger traffic on 27th May 1872, but the section to Edmonton and beyond had to wait an additional two months. It eventually opened on 22nd July 1872 and from this date the entire route was used by both passenger and freight trains.

On 4th November 1872 the City Extension opened to Bishopsgate Low Level and this served as a temporary terminus until the first part of the new Liverpool Street station was brought into use on 2nd February 1874.

From Hackney Downs the line passed through a succession of stations, all built to a standard design, largely in yellow brick, and fitted with distinctive saw-tooth platform awnings of a type then favoured by the GER.

A little beyond the new station at Edmonton, the line met the original route from Angel Road and continued along this into Enfield. The formation of the new section was double-track from the beginning, but the stretch between Lower Edmonton Junction and Enfield remained single until an additional line was brought into use on 1st August 1872.

With a frequent and reliable service of trains to entice them, more and more people were moving from inner-London to the new suburbs and soon peak-period Enfield services were filled to capacity. Such was the demand for the special 2d return tickets, that a third train was introduced in 1883 with two more following in 1890. Towards the end of the century the total had increased to seven and there was no doubt that these were necessary as the local population continued to grow at a record rate. According to the census returns, Edmonton had 23,463 inhabitants in 1881, but by 1901 the number had grown to nearly 62,000.

As the districts grew, the peak-time trains became more overcrowded, although passenger numbers started to decline when electric tram-cars were introduced in the early twentieth century. Nevertheless, the Hackney Downs - Enfield line remained busy and survived World War I without losing any of its stations. The stretch between Hackney Downs and Liverpool Street did not fair so well however, with Bishopsgate Low Level, Cambridge Heath and London Fields all succumbing to closure in 1916. Both Cambridge Heath and London Fields subsequently reopened when the man-power situation improved, but the station at Bishopsgate remained closed and was eventually largely demolished.

Because of the intense service which the line demanded at busy times, the company considered an electrification plan, but this was ruled out as being too expensive. Instead, by making some necessary alterations at principal locations, it was deemed possible to introduce a new timetable which would greatly increase the service. For just one-fortieth of the envisaged electrification cost, the number of up trains in the morning could be increased by 75%, whilst their homeward-bound equivalents in the evening would increase by 50%.

The new service was duly implemented on 12th July 1920 and was well received by passengers and press alike. To aid quick identification of the class of travel offered by each vehicle, different coloured bands were painted above the carriage windows, with yellow for First Class and blue for Second. A system of colour coding was also introduced whereby regular passengers could readily identify their train's ultimate destination, with large boards being displayed on coaches. Those for Enfield were pale blue, Palace Gates was pink and Chingford was denoted by pale yellow. These new innovations coincided with the rise in popularity of syncopated jazz music introduced from America in the previous year and the word "jazz" was seemingly on many people's lips. In a short while the term became synonymous with anything bright or indeed garish, so it was perhaps inevitable that the riot of colours displayed on the carriage sides resulted in the press describing the trains as operating the *"Jazz Service"*. Those who considered themselves to be immune to the infectious strains of the Original Dixieland Jazz Band, Lyrical Five or Queens' Dance Orchestra however, chose to refer to it rather quaintly as the *"Rainbow Service"*.

Jazz or Rainbow, the idea proved an instant success and was described as *"The last word in steam operated suburban train services"*. It was something of which the GER could be justifiably proud, but by now the company was in its final days of independence.

Above : A First Class four-wheeled coach seen beneath the overall roof of Liverpool Street station in 1920, displaying a bright yellow stripe above its windows.

Below : A non-stopping board as displayed on passenger brake vans with the introduction of the 'Jazz Service'. Down trains carried odd identification numbers whilst those on up services were even. (Both : *The Railway Gazette* 1.10.1920)

The burdens suffered during World War I had taken a heavy toll on Britain's railways and many found themselves in a poor condition, both physically and financially. Therefore an Act was passed which amalgamated the majority of companies into four major groups. Under this scheme the GER was absorbed into the new London & North Eastern Railway and officially lost its identity from 1st January 1923.

The new order was slow to impose its mark on the London suburban network however, and things remained little changed on the Enfield line.

By this time, passenger services were progressively being hauled by a class of 0-6-2T classified by the infant LNER as 'N7'. These locomotives had been introduced by the Great Eastern Railway back in 1915, but few had been constructed prior to the grouping. They proved to be ideally suited to their tasks, so the type was perpetuated by the LNER and many more were built.

For much of its earlier history, the Enfield line was served by old four-wheeled carriages, but in 1925 a new type of passenger rolling stock was introduced. Designed by Mr H.N. Gresley, the sets comprised five bodies articulated upon six bogies and became known as "quint-arts". Trains were normally formed of two sets of these and therefore comprised ten coaches. With the ample power of the N7s and new rolling stock there was little doubt that the LNER was bringing vast improvements to the route.

The early 1930s saw the installation of new passimeter booking offices at the majority of the line's stations. These were arranged so that one person could act as both booking clerk and ticket collector and therefore allow economies to be carried out on staffing levels.

During 1934 and 1935 the majority of manual signalling on the Enfield line was replaced by colour lights, although semaphores were retained at Seven Sisters. In pre-grouping days a train stopping at all stations between Liverpool Street and Enfield took around forty minutes to complete its journey, but by the second half of the 1930s this had been reduced to just thirty-four.

Despite these improvements however, the steady decline in passenger numbers instigated three decades earlier by the introduction of electric trams continued unabated. The opening of the Piccadilly Line extension towards Cockfosters scarcely helped matters, as erstwhile regular passengers made their way by bus to stations such as Turnpike Lane or Manor House then completed their journeys into town on the new fast and comfortable tube railway.

For all this the line's prospects continued to be reasonable and the level of service remained very good. Second Class travel was withdrawn at the end of 1937, but First Class lingered on until 6th October 1941 when it was withdrawn as a wartime economy measure.

As with the previous global conflict, the line weathered the ravages of World War II well, but once again the return to normality brought changes of ownership.

The War had devastated much of the network, with the parts of London served by the former GER being particularly badly affected. In other areas throughout the country the situation was depressingly similar and something had to be done to get the railways back to pre-war standards.

The only logical answer to these and other problems which were besetting the system was for the government to take control, so from 1st January 1948, the 'Big Four' companies were amalgamated into the nationalised conglomerate to be known simply as 'British Railways'.

Once again the line remained largely unaltered and apart from the fact that locomotive and carriage liveries changed and the stations received new signs, the Enfield branch retained much of its GER character.

All this was to change with electrification however, as overhead catenaries were erected along the route in the late 1950s. Apart from the scheme scotched by the "Jazz Service" of 1920, there had been other talk of electrifying the route before, but earlier plans had all foundered. Now however, the idea was to become a reality, and from 14th November 1960 6.25kV electric trains began to operate between Liverpool Street and Enfield. Unfortunately the new system suffered various teething problems, so the intended full service had to wait until 18th June 1962 until it was introduced.

The branch terminus was rebuilt a couple of years

prior to electrification, but elsewhere along the line station modifications were largely confined to minor changes carried out on platform awnings in connection with the overhead wiring. Towards the end of the decade however, an air of decrepitude was setting in and some of the station buildings began to appear rather run-down. During the same period freight facilities were withdrawn and the various depots were closed.

In the 1970s most of the stations were subjected to rationalisation with a degree of demolition taking place and, at some locations, the shortening or removal of awnings. This period also witnessed the rise of wanton and mindless vandalism, something which has escalated ever since. In some cases this has resulted in structural damage, or, perhaps to a larger extent, disfigurement by what has become known as 'graffiti'.

Under the rail privatisation scheme instigated by the Conservative government, the operation of services was transferred to the West Anglia Great Northern Railway on 5th January 1997, with the owners being Prism Rail plc. The franchise was for 7¼ years.

THE PALACE GATES BRANCH

Authorised in 1874, this 2 mile 5 furlong 4.5 chains line from Seven Sisters was intended partly to serve the needs of those wishing to visit Alexandra Palace, and this was reflected in the name given to the branch terminus. However, in reality this was located in a quiet Wood Green side street and unsuspecting passengers alighting from trains were faced with the best part of a three-quarter mile uphill walk before reaching the Palace itself.

The branch, which was double track from the outset, opened as far as Green Lanes on 1st January 1878 and was extended to Palace Gates nine months later on 7th October.

The construction of the line more or less coincided with the surrounding area being developed, so it soon started to carry commuter traffic. The 2d workmens tickets, popular with travellers on the Enfield route, were not available on the branch however, although it was possible to buy 3d returns to Liverpool Street before 7am, or 4d returns between 7am and 8am.

The hoped-for excursion traffic to Alexandra Palace never really materialised, although the line could sometimes become quite busy during bank holidays or when a special event was being held. Normally however, commuters provided the chief reason for the line's existence.

Patronage began to decline following the introduction of electric tramcars on local routes in the early twentieth century and fell even more with the opening of the Piccadilly Line through Wood Green to Arnos Grove in 1932. Nevertheless the branch soldiered on and, despite falling passenger numbers, remained open.

The tracks of the branch ended close to the Great Northern Railway north of Wood Green, but initially no physical connection between the two routes was laid. A year after the grouping however, the newly formed LNER received Parliamentary authority to join them and therefore provide a useful link for through running. For a while nothing happened, then, spurred on by the construction of a new carriage washing plant at Bounds Green, a single-track link was laid in the adjoining sidings and brought into use during 1930. This enabled carriages from the Great Eastern section to benefit from the new facilities and later witnessed a number of through excursion trains. It also proved useful for freight traffic, although from 9th July 1944 it was replaced by a better single-track connection signalled for bi-directional running.

Freight traffic had used the Palace Gates branch from the beginning, but began to decline during the 1950s as a result of competition from road hauliers. Passenger numbers also continued to dwindle and it came as no surprise when the line was proposed for closure. It was worked by steam almost to the end, but the task of hauling the last passenger train fell to a diesel locomotive, with official closure taking place from 7th January 1963. Freight traffic lingered a little longer, but towards the end of 1964 had virtually ceased.

The majority of track was subsequently lifted, leaving just a little at the country end of the former terminus which was retained for a while as part of the Bounds Green sidings complex.

ALEXANDRA PARK BRANCH.—Great Eastern.

Liverpool Street to Palace Gates (Wood Green), at 7 40, 8 10, 8 43 (not stopping at Bethnal Green, Cambridge Heath, or London Fields), 9 12, 9 43, 9 52, and 10 40 mrn. ; every half-hour from 11 10 mrn. to 3 40 aft., 4 11, 4 43, 5 8, 5 45, 6 12, 6 44 ; every half-hour from 7 10 to 9 40, and at 10 21, 11, and 11 40 aft. SUNDAYS at 8 55, 9 55, and 10 41 mrn. ; 12 40, 1 10, and every hour from 1 55, to 9 55, and at 10 41 aft

Palace Gates to Liverpool Street at 7 5, 7 35, 8 1, 8 30 (not stopping at Seven Sisters, Stamford Hill, Hackney Downs, Cambridge Heath, Bethnal Green, or Bishopsgate), 8 37, 9 7, and 9 36 mrn. ; every half-hour from 10 5 mrn. to 9 5 aft. and at 9 42, 10 25, and 11 5 aft. SUNDAYS at 8 20, 9 20, 10 5, and 10 35 mrn. ; 12 35, and every hour from 1 20 to 9 20, and at 10 5 aft. The Trains call at Bishopsgate 2, Bethnal Green 5, Cambridge Heath 8, London Fields 10, Hackney Downs 13, Rectory Road 16. Stoke Newington (for Abney Park) 18 Stamford Hill 21, Seven Sisters (Tottenham) 24 West Green 26, Green Lanes 30 arriving at Palace Gates 32 minutes after leaving Liverpool Street.

Fenchurch Street to Palace Gates (Wood Green) every hour from 7 53 mrn. to 9 53 aft. Palace Gates to Fenchurch Street every hour from 7 13 to 11 13 mrn.; 12 13, 1 11, 2 13, 3 13. 4 13, 5 13. 6 11. 7 13, 8 11, and 9 13 aft. The Trains call at St'epney 6, Burdett Road 8, Bow Road 10, Stratford 15, Lea Bridge 22, Seven Sisters 28, West Green, 30, Green Lanes 34, arriving at Palace Gates 36 minutes after leaving Fenchurch Street.

1880

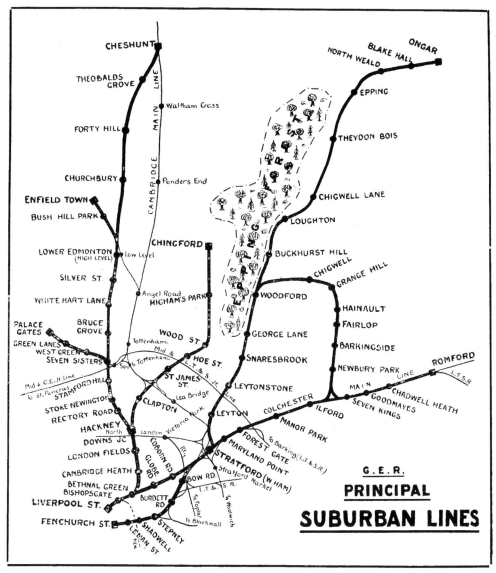

Railway Magazine December 1907

PASSENGER SERVICES

When the first section of the new line to Enfield opened on 27th May 1872, trains only operated between Bishopsgate and Stoke Newington. From the beginning special 2d workmen tickets were available for use on the 5.20am and 6.20am departures from Stoke Newington, both of which called at all stations en-route.

Trains were extended into Enfield two months later, but for a while it was not possible to operate a full service because of restricted accommodation at Bishopsgate. Matters improved with the opening of the Liverpool Street terminus however and by 1876 Enfield was served by four trains an hour outside of the peak periods, although two of these reversed at White Hart Lane.

Demand for 2d return tickets was such that the number of trains on which they were valid steadily rose during the next two decades until by 1898 they totalled seven. Passengers using these had to depart before 7am but could return on any train leaving Liverpool Street after 4pm, Mondays to Fridays, or mid-day on Saturdays.

By 1900 it was also possible to purchase 3d returns and depart between 7am and 7.30am, or else pay half the standard fare to arrive at Liverpool Street no later than 8am.

The basic Enfield service was reduced to half-hourly as a result of tramway competition, but the route remained busy in the peaks and in 1907 the branch terminus boasted six departures for Liverpool Street between 7am and 8am. The normal journey time for stopping trains during this period was forty minutes, but some semi-fasts completed the run in just twenty-seven.

The Palace Gates branch was also provided with frequent Liverpool Street through services, although since 1st June 1887 these had been joined by trains to and from North Woolwich, which operated by way of South Tottenham. Seven years earlier, from 1st January 1880, the line had seen through workings from Fenchurch Street, but these ceased after 1st September 1880, when the trains were diverted by way of the new 'Limehouse Curve' to serve Blackwall instead of Fenchurch Street. The service proved very short lived, as it last operated on 28th February 1881, but the slightly later link with North Woolwich remained until the Palace Gates branch closed in 1963.

The opening of what is now known as the Southbury Loop in 1891 brought a few extra trains to the section of Enfield line south of Lower Edmonton, but traffic was never brisk and the loop was twice subjected to periods of closure, with the second lasting for over forty years.

The "*Jazz*" of 1920 brought changes to both the Enfield and Palace Gates lines, with the latter being served in off-peak hours by a thirty-minute interval shuttle which plied between the branch terminus and Seven Sisters. Throughout the week, off-peak services on the Enfield line ran every ten minutes and became even more frequent during rush hours. In the evening, one hour saw nine departures from Liverpool Street to Enfield and three to Palace Gates, therefore providing the section between the City and Seven Sisters with a total of twelve trains.

By the time war broke out in 1939 Sunday services had been reduced to half-hourly, and the same interval was introduced to off-peak trains in the early 1940s. Through services on the Palace Gates branch had also been withdrawn, but the shuttling auto-trains carried on until 6th July 1942 when they were taken off in the interest of economy. All that now remained on the branch was the service to and from North Woolwich, although after hostilities ended, the Seven Sisters shuttle was re-introduced on 31st May 1948, only to cease completely from 15th January 1951.

The reopening of the long-moribund Southbury Loop in 1960 brought more trains to part of the Enfield line, although, for a while, these ran non-stop between Lower Edmonton and Liverpool Street.

The full electric service introduced on the Enfield line on 18th June 1962, revived the old off-peak intervals of a train every ten minutes, with those calling at all stations completing journeys in twenty-nine minutes and semi-fasts in twenty-five.

The Palace Gates branch closed soon after, having been served by trains to and from the North Woolwich line until the end.

The ten-minute frequency of Enfield line trains failed to generate the anticipated amount of patronage, so was reduced to an interval of twenty minutes in the summer of 1965. Three years later, on 1st September 1968, the new Victoria Line tube opened to Walthamstow and included a station at Seven Sisters. Interchange facilities were made available and Southbury Loop trains began to call whereas they had previously passed through non-stop. Unfortunately, the down side to this development was that passenger numbers on the stretch between Seven Sisters and Liverpool Street began to decline.

In an attempt to bring more public awareness to the route, the Greater London Council funded a scheme which resulted in increased frequencies. Starting on 3rd October 1983, the Enfield line was provided with four trains an hour from 10.00 until 16.00, Monday to Friday, and 19.00 on Saturday. It was promoted on leaflets and posters as 'The Jazz Service', but the origin of this must have been lost on the majority of passengers who had little interest in railway history. Frequencies on the section south of what was then Lower Edmonton were even better, as the addition of Southbury Loop workings resulted in a gap of just ten minutes between trains. Sadly the results were disappointing and the inevitable reductions came after 12th May 1986.

The timetable introduced in September 2003 showed a basic half-hourly weekday pattern on the Enfield line, increased of course at peak times. Sunday trains were hourly, although trains ran at approximately thirty minutes intervals over the stretch between Liverpool Street and Edmonton Green, because of the additional Southbury line services.

HACKNEY DOWNS

1. We start our exploration of the 1872 Great Eastern route to Enfield with this view of the approach to Hackney Downs taken around 1911. The photographer was positioned on a signal post and was looking north towards the station. The bridge in the foreground carries the GER over the North London Railway Dalston Junction - Poplar line and a short section of track is just visible at the bottom left corner. The houses are facing onto both sides of Spurstowe Road, whilst in front of those to the right we have a rare view of the passenger footway which once linked Hackney Downs station with Hackney on the NLR. The construction of this link was approved by the company's Ways and Works Committee on 1st April 1884 and it opened on 1st December 1885. Both companies agreed to shared the costs, including ticket collection, but it is understood that the interchange booking office which served the facility was staffed solely by the GER. To provide a link between the platforms and footway, a footbridge was provided, although this had to be replaced when the formation was widened in 1894. (British Rail)

The Ordnance Survey map of 1913 shows the station and its immediate surroundings as they were around the time that the photograph on the previous page was taken.

Hackney Downs, located 2 miles 78 chains from Liverpool Street, opened on 27th May 1872 with two platforms serving two tracks. It was soon enlarged however, as from 1st June 1876 a pair of through lines were added.

The premises then remained little altered, apart from the addition of the footway connection with the NLR, until the formation between there and Bethnal Green was widened in the 1890s. The contract for this was awarded to the firm of Holme & King in June 1892 and was completed towards the end of 1894. Under this new arrangement, the fast lines were on the east side of the route and the slow lines on the west. A replacement footbridge was approved by the Ways and Works Committee on 30th July 1895 and constructed by the Thames Ironworks.

There were two signal boxes, Hackney Downs North, which stood a little beyond the country end of the down local platform and Hackney Downs South, which can be seen on the map on the down side, just to the north of Wilton Road. When colour-light signalling was introduced the latter box was declared redundant and was closed on 17th November 1935, although a ground frame was installed to operate the adjoining crossover.

The long covered footway linking the GER with the NLR is also visible on the map, together with the interchange booking office, which is represented by a small rectangle on the up side, just south of Spurstowe Road. The western end of Hackney NLR station can be seen near the right hand edge.

The sidings on the left belong to Graham Road goods depot, which although owned by the GER, was reached by means of the North London line. This depot functioned from May 1894 until 4th October 1965.

2. Here we have a pre-grouping view of the station, looking north from the up local platform, with the 1895 footbridge prominent in the foreground. According to the noted London railway historian H.V. Borley, the "Junction" part of the name was dropped in 1896, but it is known to have survived on nameboards at least into the early 1930s. (The Lens of Sutton Collection)

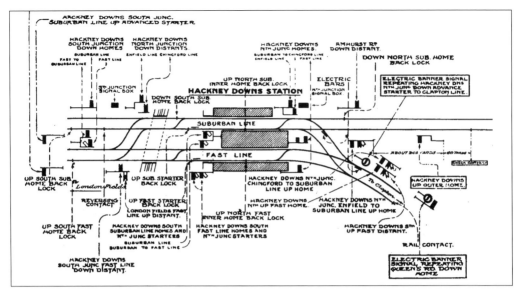

Here we see a signalling diagram of the station dating from the introduction of the *'Jazz Service'* in 1920. (The Railway Gazette)

3. A young locoman smiles for the camera as Class N7/5 0-6-2T No. 69666 pauses at the station on 4th October 1954 with an Enfield Town - Liverpool Street train formed of a single 'quint-art' set. The covered footway link to the former NLR Hackney station closed on 15th May 1944 when the Broad Street - Poplar passenger service was withdrawn, but its associated footbridge survived, albeit minus its roofing. The bridge had now become rather superfluous, as the platforms were also linked by a subway closer to the northern end, and it had disappeared by 1958. (Photographer unknown)

4. Class N7/3 0-6-2T No. 69726 stands beneath the overhead wiring as she pauses at Platform 4 with a train for Enfield Town around 1960. (Norfolk Railway Society)

5. This view looks north from the central island platform soon after electrification. Interestingly, the buildings erected at the time of the 1894 widening were provided with canopy valances typical of their era, but that on the down local side retained one of the type employed in the 1870s. The lamp posts and attendant 'totem' signs were soon to be replaced by fluorescent strip lighting. (Norfolk Railway Society)

6. During the re-signalling of 1935, the old North signal box was retained, but was renamed 'Hackney Downs Junction'. This was fitted with a McKenzie & Holland frame comprising thirty-one levers. On 28th/29th May 1960, it was replaced by a new power box of BR 'Type 18' on the north end of the island platform which boasted a Westinghouse 'NX' panel and was provided with a prominent sun baffle. Here we see the two cabins, with the original on the left and its replacement to the right. The nameboard propped against the wall suggests that the photograph was taken just prior to opening. (The Lens of Sutton Collection)

7. The box was brought into use overnight on 28th/29th May 1960 and is seen soon after with a train for Liverpool Street, led by unit No.305 approaching from the Rectory Road direction. Notice that the earlier cabin has now been demolished. (J. Richards)

8. Down in the subway leading from the booking hall to the stairways, vitreous enamel signs once directed passengers to their relevant platforms. That seen here pointed towards the down local side and, when recorded in December 1965, still included Palace Gates, even though the branch had already been closed for nearly three years. The sign was destined to last for a while longer, although the reference to Palace Gates was later obscured by paint. (J.E. Connor)

9. This view, which dates from around 1969, was taken from the south end of Platform 4 and shows that few changes had taken place since electrification apart from the installation of new platform lighting. (I. Baker)

10. The station underwent a programme of improvements in the early 1980s, including the erection of a new street level building and partial replacement of canopy valances. This view was taken from the north end of platform 4 in July 1984 and shows a new section of valancing on the island with the 1960 signal box beyond. This cabin remained in use until May 2001 when its work was taken over by the Liverpool Street Control Centre. (The South Chingford Railway Circle)

11. A northward view from March 2002 shows unit 315 856 departing for Chingford, having just called at platform 2. Although the canopy valancing on this side of the station was renewed in the early 1980s, the attendant ironwork is still of GER origin, as are the platform buildings. In early 2004, the platform serving the down local line still retained its 1870s style valancing as shown in photograph No. 5. (C.D. Connor)

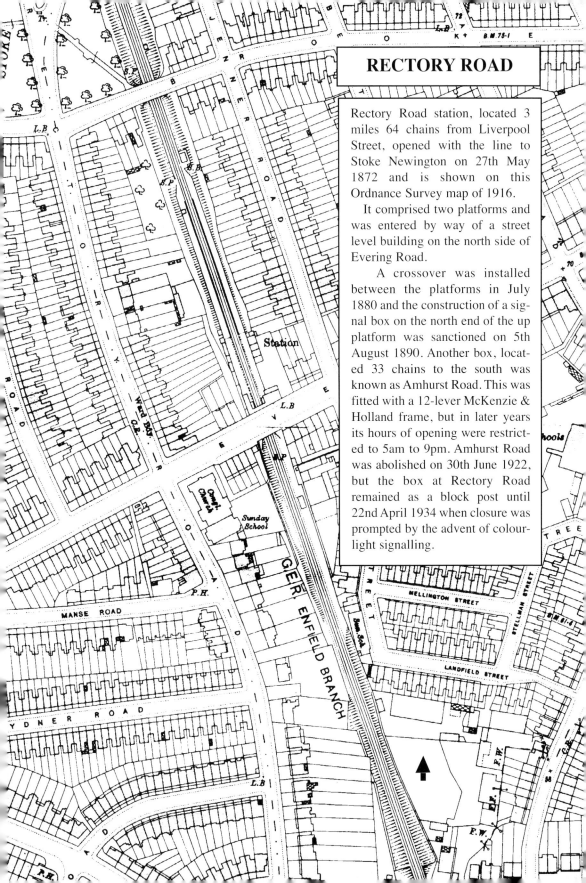

RECTORY ROAD

Rectory Road station, located 3 miles 64 chains from Liverpool Street, opened with the line to Stoke Newington on 27th May 1872 and is shown on this Ordnance Survey map of 1916.

It comprised two platforms and was entered by way of a street level building on the north side of Evering Road.

A crossover was installed between the platforms in July 1880 and the construction of a signal box on the north end of the up platform was sanctioned on 5th August 1890. Another box, located 33 chains to the south was known as Amhurst Road. This was fitted with a 12-lever McKenzie & Holland frame, but in later years its hours of opening were restricted to 5am to 9pm. Amhurst Road was abolished on 30th June 1922, but the box at Rectory Road remained as a block post until 22nd April 1934 when closure was prompted by the advent of colour-light signalling.

12.   An up train is seen arriving at the station around 1904. Originally there was little in the way of specific waiting accommodation on the down side, but this was remedied when a ladies room was approved by the GER Ways and Works Committee on 17th August 1880. A porters room was added in 1897, but otherwise little happened until 21st November 1905 when authority was given to extend both platforms to make them suitable for longer trains. Originally illuminated by oil lamps, it was reported in May 1906 that Rectory Road was among a small group of stations to have recently been fitted with incandescent gas lighting. (Commercial postcard / P. Laming Collection)

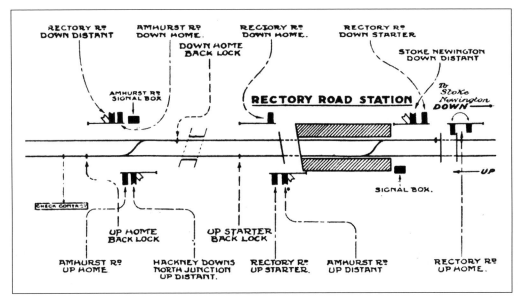

This is a signalling diagram of 1920 which shows the station together with the signal box at Amhurst Road which lay to its south. (The Railway Gazette)

13. This view looks north in the early 1950s and includes the wooden signal box at the far end of the up platform. Although this had closed in 1934 it was retained for a number of years and used as a permanent way hut. When in use for its intended purpose it was fitted with a 12-lever McKenzie & Holland frame. (Stations UK)

14. The general appearance of the station remained little altered for over nine decades as this view taken around the time of electrification shows. We are standing at the north end of the down platform, looking towards Hackney Downs. The overhead wires are up, but vintage lamp posts are still in position, along with 'totem' style name tablets. (The Lens of Sutton Collection)

15. By the mid-1960s, the station was beginning to look rather run-down and part of the down side awning had been removed along with its supporting wall. In this view we are looking south and can see a green liveried EMU approaching from the opposite side of the Evering Road bridge. (J.E. Connor)

16. Despite the rationalisation of the down side awning, its counterpart on the opposite platform remained in fairly good order, although, as can be seen in this southwards view, even this was looking grimy and unkempt. In the early hours of 9th December 1972 a fire broke out and the damage was serious enough for the station to remain closed until 17th January 1973. The old buildings now entered a period of terminal decline. (J.E. Connor)

17. By 1983 when this photograph was taken, the street level building was out of use and access was by means of an adjoining gateway. Boarded-up and derelict it looked to all the world like a closed station, with only the British Rail double-arrow logo and the nameboard, which is thought to have originated on one of the platforms, to indicate that the place was in fact still open. (J.E. Connor)

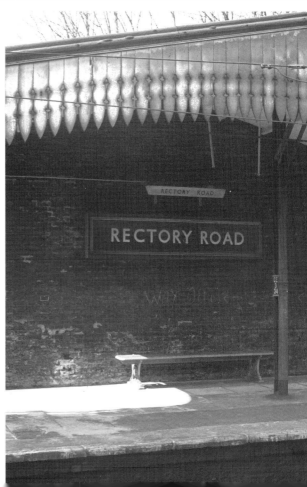

18. Despite the surrounding desolation, a vintage blue enamel running-in board could still be seen beneath the awning on the down side. This view looks across from the up platform in 1983. (J.E. Connor)

19. Although it still sheltered its nostalgic nameboard, the down side canopy was clearly nearing the end of its days. This is another view taken in 1983, when complete rebuilding was becoming imminent. (J.E. Connor)

20. We take our leave of Rectory Road with this view taken from the down platform looking towards central London in February 2004. The station was completely rebuilt during 1984-5, with three-quarters of the costs being supplied under the government funded Urban Aid Programme. (J.E. Connor)

STOKE NEWINGTON

The station can be seen near the top of this Ordnance Survey map of 1916. It opened on 27th May 1872 and for nearly two months served as a temporary terminus. It is located 4 miles 17 chains from Liverpool Street and was constructed in brick lined cutting. The two flights of steps leading up to the thoroughfare above the platforms towards the London end (Cazenove Road) provided a supplementary means of access approved by the GER Ways & Works Committee in February 1909. The signal box, located at the south end of the up platform, was provided with a 13-lever McKenzie & Holland frame and remained in use until 22nd April 1934 when it closed as part of the colour-light signalling scheme.

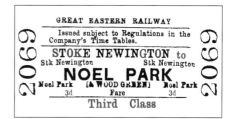

21.   The street level building was constructed largely in yellow brick and was provided with a forecourt for cabs and other waiting vehicles. In this photograph, we are looking towards the entrance during the first decade of the twentieth century. (Commercial postcard / P. Laming Collection)

22.   In another view from the same era, the photographer was standing on the up platform looking north as a train for Liverpool Street steams beneath the road bridge and street level building. (Commercial postcard / P. Laming Collection)

23. Here we view a similar scene, but this time from the down side. Behind the gentleman in the centre we can see the station bookstall which was authorised towards the end of 1898 and probably opened in the following year. Although the station's appearance remained largely unaltered, the premises were subject to various additions over the years, including a milk-churn lift provided by the East Ferry Road Engineering Company in 1888-9 and a ladies waiting room in 1891. Another change came in 1905-6 when the platforms were extended to accommodate longer trains. (Commercial postcard / P. Laming Collection)

LIVERPOOL STREET, WALTHAMSTOW, TOTTENHAM, EDMONTON, and ENFIELD.—G.E.

Enfield—From Liverpool Street every ¼-hour from........	7 25 mrn to 11 55 aft —Week Days. 8 55 mrn to 10 25 mrn } Sundays. 12 55 aft to 10 55 aft	Enfield—From Enfield every ¼-hour from ..	6 41 mrn to 11 11 aft —Week Days. 8 11 mrn to 10 11 mrn } Sundays. 12 41 aft to 10 11 aft
Tottenham (White Hart Lane)— FrmLiverpool Street every ¼-hour from ..	7 40 mrn to 8 40 aft —Week Days. 2 10 aft to 10 40 aft —Sundays.	Tottenham (White Hart Lane)— Fm White Hart Lane every ¼-hour from ..	7 7 mrn to 8 7 aft —Week Days. 1 37 aft to 10 7 aft —Sundays.
Walthamstow. — FrmLiverpool Street every ¼-hour from ..	7 33 mrn to 8 33 aft } Week Days. 8 33 mrn to 10 33 mrn 1 3 aft to 11 3 aft } Sundays.	Walthamstow—From Wood Street every ¼-hour from	7 4 mrn to 8 34 aft } Week Days. 9 11 aft to 11 41 aft 8 4 mrn to 10 34 mrn } Sundays 1 4 aft to 10 34 aft

Extra on Week Days.—Walthamstow to Liverpool Street at 5, 6, 8 19, 8 45, 9 19, and 9 47 mrn.; also at 4 49, 5 49, and 3 49 aft. Saturdays excepted, and 2 19 and 3 19 aft. Saturdays only; returning at 5 33, 6 33, 8 48, 9 15, 9 48, and 10½ mrn.; also at 5 17, 6 18, and 7 18 aft. Saturdays excepted, and 2 48 and 3 48 aft. Saturdays only. Enfield to Liverpool Street at 4 55, 5 20, 6, 6 56, 7 26, 7 56, 8 26, and 8 56 mrn.; 1 35 (Saturdays only), 3 52 (except Saturdays), 5 56, 6 26, 6 56, 7 26, and 7 56 aft.; returning at 5 45, 6 8, 6 45, and 10 mrn.; 5 10, 5 40, 6 10, 6 40, 7 10, 7 40, 8 10, and 8 40 aft.
Enfield to Liverpool Street (1&2 class) at 9 21 mrn.; returning at 2 18 (Sats. only, 1&2 class) and 4 38 (except Sats.) aft., alling at Bishopsgate, Hackney Downs, Seven Sisters, Bruce Grove, White Hart Lane, Silver Street, and Edmonton.

June 1876

24.   Stoke Newington station remained little altered well into the British Railways era, as is apparent from this photograph which dates from the 1950s. Standing at the up platform is a train from Enfield Town to Liverpool Street which is formed of 'quint-art' stock and headed by Class N7/5 0-6-2T No. 69665. Locomotives working these services generally ran chimney-first out of London and bunker-first on the return.   (RAS Marketing)

25.   Apart from the addition of overhead wiring, the 1960s continued to bring little change to the premises. This view looks north from the up platform and shows the distinctive awnings which were of a type favoured by the Great Eastern Railway for a number of stations in the 1870s and 80s.   (Stations UK)

26. We stand on the down platform looking south during the 1960s and, in the middle distance, see one of the gated flight of stairs which, from 1909, provided access to Cazenove Road. (The Lens of Sutton Collection)

27. The following decade saw a start being made on the demolition of the old buildings. We remain on the down side, but it is now 1973 and we witness the early stages of canopy removal. The work was completed during 1974-5. (J.E. Connor)

28. As part of the station alterations undertaken in the 1970s the original street level building was demolished and replaced by one of new design. Here this is seen in July 1982. (The South Chingford Railway Circle)

29. Before leaving Stoke Newington, let us pause on the down platform and look northwards to see the station as it appeared in February 2004. The stairway roofing disappeared along with the original canopies during the 1970s, but short sections of new awning were erected as part of the rebuilding scheme to provide shelter for waiting passengers. (J.E. Connor)

STOKE NEWINGTON GOODS

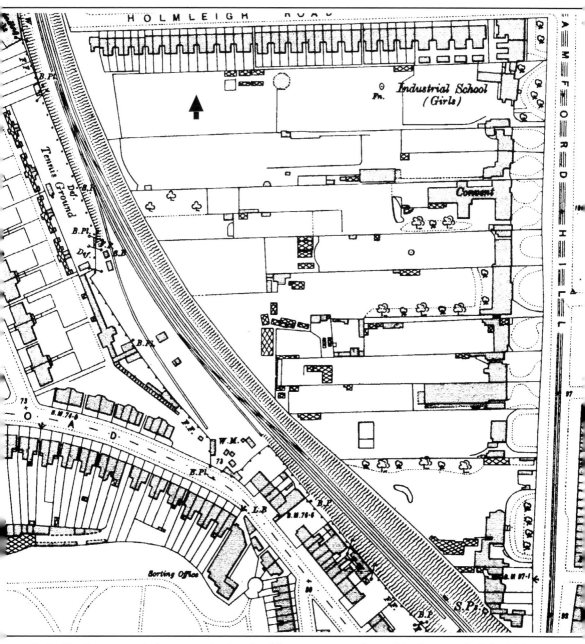

Stoke Newington goods depot was sited north of the passenger station and is shown to the left of this Ordnance Survey map of 1916. It opened in December 1872 and was located to the west of the forma-tion. The depot comprised a couple of sidings, which were separated by a cartage road, and these were reached by means of a loop adjoining the down line. Access to this was controlled by Manor Road Sidings signal box which initially accommodated fourteen levers within its McKenzie & Holland frame, but the number was increased to seventeen in 1921. The box was down-graded to the status of a ground frame on 22nd April 1934 and served as such until the goods yard closed on 7th December 1964.

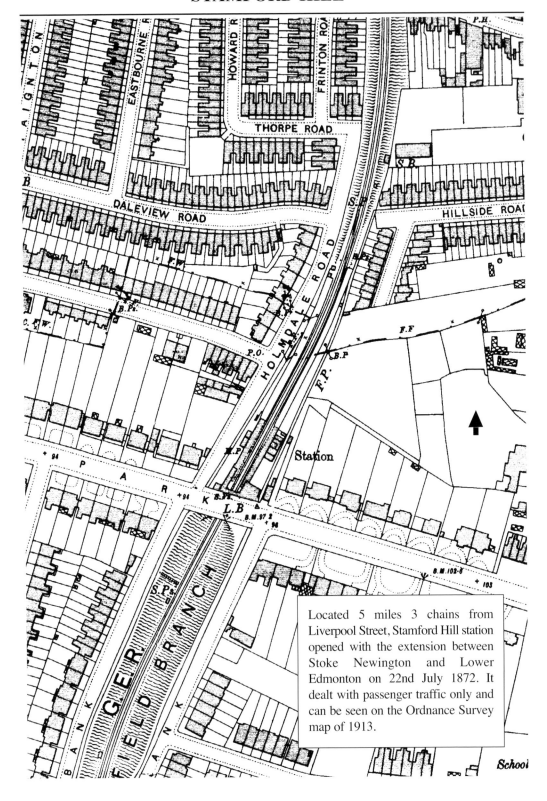

Located 5 miles 3 chains from Liverpool Street, Stamford Hill station opened with the extension between Stoke Newington and Lower Edmonton on 22nd July 1872. It dealt with passenger traffic only and can be seen on the Ordnance Survey map of 1913.

30. When opened, the station served a developing residential suburb comprising a few select villas with large gardens. In this view we see the street level building in tree-lined Amhurst Park as it appeared in the early years of the twentieth century. (Commercial postcard / P. Laming Collection)

31. Moving a little closer we have a fine view of the street level building in Great Eastern days, showing the style adopted for most stations along the route. At the time it was still largely in original condition, although the coal office seen on the right may have been added in 1882. (The Lens of Sutton Collection)

32. Still in the pre-grouping era we stand near the north end of the up platform and look towards Enfield Town. In the middle distance can be seen the wooden signal box which accommodated twenty-two levers in its Dutton Trigger frame and remained in use until 22nd April 1934. (C.K. Hoser Collection)

LONDON, WALTHAMSTOW, CHINGFORD, PALACE GATES, and ENFIELD TOWN.—G. E.

Down.	mrn	mrn	mrn	mrn	mrn	mrn	mrn	mrn	mrn	mrn	mrn	mrn	mrn	mrn	mrn	mrn	mrn	mrn	mrn	mrn	mrn	mrn	mrn	mrn	mrn	mrn
Liverpool St. d	450	550	620	627	633	6 36	6 47	6 53	7 2	7 25	732	749	755	8 8	818	825	829	836	846	857	9 0	9 4	921	9 26	9 31	935	9 42	9 55	9 58
Bishopsgate ..	452	552	622	...	635	6 38	6 49	6 55	4 7	7 27	734	751	757	8 5	815	827	831	838	848	...	9 2	9 6	...	9 28	9 33	937	9 44	9 57	10 0
Bethnal Green	455	555	625	...	638	6 41	6 52	6 53	7 7	7 30	737	751	8 0	8 8	818	830	834	841	851	9 1	9 5	9 9	...	9 31	9 37	940	9 47	10 0	10 3
Cambrdge Hth	458	558	628	...	641	6 44	6 55	7	1 7	10 7	33	740	757	8 3	811	821	833	837	...	854	...	9 8	912	...	9 34	9 40	943	9 50	...	10 6
London Fields	5 0	6 0	630	...	643	6 46	6 57	7	3 7	12 7	35	742	759	8 5	813	823	835	839	844	856	...	910	914	...	9 36	9 42	945	9 52	...	10 8
Hackney Dwn	5 3	6 3	633	...	646	6 49	7 0	7	6 7	15 7	38	745	8 2	8 8	816	826	838	844	847	859	9 7	913	919	...	9 39	9 45	948	9 55	10 6	1011
Clapton	...	...	635	...	649	...	...	...	7 18	...	748	...	...	819	...	...	847	...	...	...	922	...	...	...	951	...	...	...
Wlthmstw *	...	...	640	...	653	...	...	...	7 22	...	752	...	...	823	...	...	851	...	...	...	926	...	...	...	955	...	...	...
„ Hoe St..	...	...	642	...	655	...	...	...	7 24	...	754	...	...	925	...	...	853	...	...	...	928	...	...	...	957	...	...	...
„ Wood St.	...	...	645	...	658	...	...	...	7 27	...	757	...	...	828	...	...	856	...	...	...	931	...	...	...	100	...	...	...
Hale End....	...	...	...	...	7 3	...	...	...	...	...	8 2	...	...	833	...	...	...	...	...	...	936	...	...	...	105	...	...	...
Chingford *	...	...	...	...	7 7	...	...	...	...	...	8 6	...	...	837	...	...	...	...	...	...	940	...	...	...	109	...	...	...
Rectory Road..	5 6	6 6	6	...	...	6 52	7	3 7	9	Woo	7 41	...	8 5	811	...	829	...	850	9 2	910	916	...	...	9 42	9 48	...	9 58	10 9	1014
StkNewington	5 8	6 8	...	639	...	6 54	7	5 7	11	to	7 43	...	8 7	813	...	831	...	852	9 4	912	918	...	...	9 44	9 50	...	10 0	1011	1016
Stamford Hill	511	611	...	...	...	6 57	7	8 7	14	St.	7 46	...	810	816	...	834	...	855	9 7	...	921	...	...	9 47	9 53	...	10 3	1014	1019
Seven Sisters..	514	614	...	643	...	7 0	7	11 7	17	Liverpool	7 49	...	813	819	...	837	844	...	858	911	916	924	...	...	9 50	9 56	...	10 6	1017	1022
West Green..	...	...	...	...	...	7 7	...	...	...	not stopping.	...	...	815	...	...	839	...	...	913	...	926	...	...	...	10 8	...	...	1024
GreenLanes	...	...	...	...	...	7 11	...	...	...	...	...	819	...	843	...	...	917	...	930	...	...	...	1012	...	...	1026
Palace Gts	...	...	...	...	...	7 13	...	...	...	...	...	821	...	845	...	...	919	...	932	...	...	...	1014	...	...	1030
Bruce Grove..	516	616	...	...	...	7	2 7	13 7	19	...	7 51	...	821	...	847	...	9 0	...	918	...	...	...	9 52	9 58	...	...	1019	...
WhiteHartLn.	519	619	...	647	...	7	5 7	16 7	22	...	7 54	...	824	...	850	...	9 3	...	921	...	942	9 55	10 1	...	...	1022	...
Silver Street	522	622	...	...	...	7	8 7	19 7	25	...	7 57	...	827	...	853	...	9 6	...	924	...	9 58	10 4	...	...	1026	...
LwerEdmontn	525	625	...	651	...	7 11	7 22	7 28	...	...	8 0	...	830	...	855	...	9 9	...	927	...	947	10 1	10 7	...	...	1028	...
Bush HillPark	...	628	...	...	...	7 14	7 25	7 31	...	...	...	...	833	...	858	...	912	...	...	...	...	10 4	1010	...	...	1031	...
Enfield Town a	530	631	...	656	...	7 17	7 28	7 34	...	...	8 5	...	836	...	9 1	...	915	...	932	...	952	10 7	1013	...	...	1034	...

February 1890

33. As with most of the stations along the route, Stamford Hill remained little changed until long after nationalisation, although in earlier days, waiting rooms were added during 1879 and a down side ladies' room followed in 1880. This photograph was taken from the north end of the down side soon after the erection of the overhead wiring, whilst work was under way on the installation of new lighting. (The Lens of Sutton Collection)

34. From a similar viewpoint we see Class N7/3 0-6-2T No. 69685 arriving with a peak hour train from Liverpool Street to Enfield towards the end of steam days. (The Lens of Sutton Collection)

35.   Pointing his camera in the opposite direction, the photographer recorded an N7 hauling an up train from Enfield Town into the station.   (The Lens of Sutton Collection)

36.   The street level building on the north side of Amhurst Park underwent a few changes over the years but still retained its original character. This view dates from the early 1970s, when white-on-blue signs, such as that seen above the doorway, were fast becoming rare, as they fell foul of the British Rail corporate image introduced in the previous decade.   (J.L. Crook)

37. The 1970s saw the general decline of the old station buildings along the route, and Stamford Hill was no exception. This view shows the up platform after its awning had been drastically shortened. (M. Foley)

38. The station was subsequently modernised, but the original street level building was retained and equipped with a new ticket office in 1979. Here it is seen around three years later and apart from a few minor changes it still retained much of its original fabric in February 2004. (The South Chingford Railway Circle)

39. Although the former GER street level building was retained, the surviving platform level structures were swept away and replaced by new shelters in 1984. This view was taken from the southern end of the station in February 2004 and shows passengers about to board unit No. 315 845 which is working a service to Liverpool Street. (J.E. Connor)

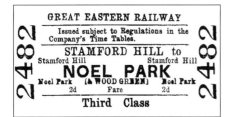

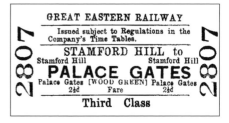

SEVEN SISTERS

40. We stand just north of the junction at Seven Sisters and look towards the station possibly around the time of World War I. The Palace Gates branch platforms can be seen on the left, whilst the original premises stand on the right. (Commercial postcard / P. Laming collection)

The Ordnance Survey map of 1894, reproduced overleaf, shows us Seven Sisters station, located 5 miles 50 chains from Liverpool Street, with the line to Enfield Town heading in the centre and the branch to Palace Gates to the left. When opened on 22nd July 1872, it comprised just two platforms serving the Enfield route, but a further pair were brought into use on 1st January 1878 when trains began working over the first section of the Palace Gates branch.

Immediately north of the Enfield line platforms can be seen the private sidings which were built to serve the premises of the Lager Beer Brewing Company. These first appeared in the GER Locomotive and Ways & Works Committee minutes of 4th July 1882 and were probably laid soon after. The brewery subsequently underwent various changes of name and ceased beer production in 1903. The building then became known as the Imperial Cold Stores and subsequently shared the sidings with the Tottenham Urban District Council. The Imperial Cold Stores was destroyed by a 'doodlebug' in World War II and the disused sidings were subsequently lifted around 1953.

At the base of the map, we can see the start of a spur, leading to the right, which provided a connection with South Tottenham on today's Barking - Gospel Oak route. The spur opened to freight in 1879 and passengers from 1st January 1880 and allowed the operation of services such as that which linked North Woolwich to Palace Gates. According to the GER Board of Directors minutes dated 19th June 1878, the spoil used to construct the spur's embankment had been transferred from West Green on the Palace Gates branch where it had been excavated to form a cutting.

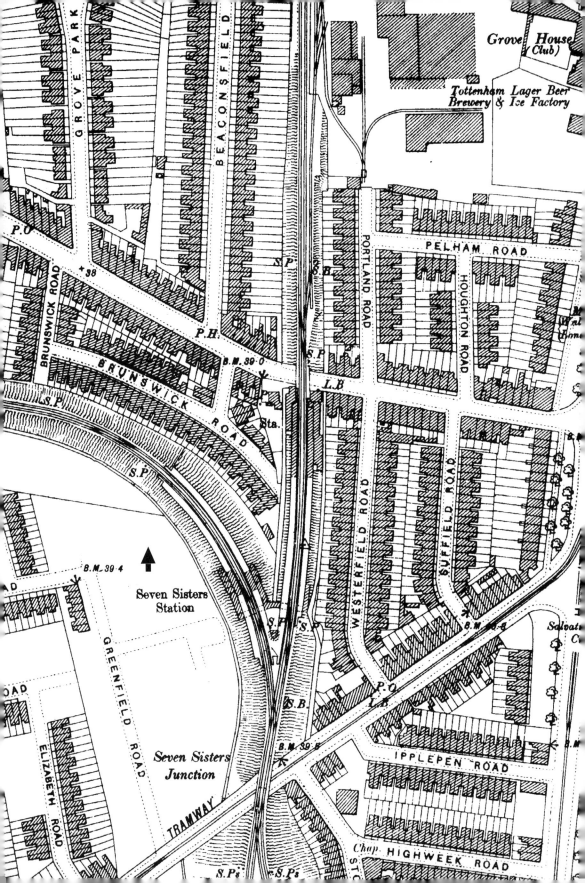

Grove House
(Club)

Tottenham Lager Beer
Brewery & Ice Factory

GROVE PARK

BEACONSFIELD

PELHAM ROAD

PORTLAND ROAD

HOUGHTON ROAD

P.O

+ 38

S.P.

S.B.

BRUNSWICK ROAD

P.H.

B.M. 39·0

S.P.

L.B.

P.

Sta.

S.P.

BRUNSWICK ROAD

S.P.

SUFFIELD ROAD

WESTERFIELD ROAD

B.M. 39·4

Seven Sisters
Station

GREENFIELD ROAD

ELIZABETH ROAD

Seven Sisters
Junction

S.P. S.P.

B.M. 39·

S.B.

P.O.

B.M. 39·

IPPLEPEN ROAD

Salvation
C

TRAMWAY

Chap. HIGHWEEK ROAD

S.Ps   S.Ps

41. In this view we are looking north along the Enfield line platforms in the 1930s. The main buildings, which can be seen at the far end, incorporated stairways which led to and from the entrance in West Green Road, and were of the same basic design as the other 1872 stations elsewhere along the route. To the left we see the entrance to a stairway used by passengers wishing to access the Palace Gates branch, with its directional sign a little further to the right. Soon after the branch opened the GER decided to erect such a sign and, in February 1879, acquired quotes for both vitreous enamel and painted versions. The latter proved considerably cheaper to produce, so not surprisingly one of these was duly commissioned.

Comparatively few alterations were undertaken on the Enfield side of the station for many years, although the height of the rear wall on the up side was raised by fifteen inches in 1883 and a 10 cwt milk lift added around 1902. More significant changes were to come soon after however, when an additional entrance from Birstall Road was authorised in July 1905 and opened the following year. Around the same time, the Ways & Works Committee approved the lengthening of the platforms at their southern end and the results of this are visible in the foreground. The Birstall Road entrance remained in use until World War II, when it closed on 6th July 1942. (The Lens of Sutton Collection)

42. In July 1920 the GER introduced a push-pull shuttle service which operated between Seven Sisters and Palace Gates, worked from the outset by 2-4-2Ts of the Y65 class, or F7s as they were known in LNER days. One of these, No. 8306, is shown here, having just arrived at the up branch platform with a three-car train formed of clerestory roofed carriages on 20th October 1936. Originally formed of two vehicles only, this set was initially brought to London for working the Churchbury Loop, but made its debut on the Palace Gates branch around 1926 and remained there until the shuttles were suspended in 1942. It returned in 1948 and stayed until 1951 when it was trans-ferred to a line in rural Essex. (H.F. Wheeller / R.S. Carpenter Photos)

43. Here we see the driving end of one of the two-car push-pull sets used on the branch since 1920. The number of the vehicle is unclear, but above the buffer on the left it displays the legend *Palace Gates Push & Pull Auto Train No. 2*. The photograph was taken at Seven Sisters in 1950. (R.A.P. Cogger)

44. Remaining on the branch platforms we observe Class an N7 0-6-2T, thought to be No 69636, as she passes the up side with a train of coal wagons in the 1950s. (R.A.P. Cogger)

45. The London end of the down branch platform provided a good vantage point for watching the trains on both the Enfield and Palace Gates lines. In this view an N7 enters the station bunker-first with a train from North Woolwich and passes Seven Sisters Junction signal box which accommodated forty-eight levers within a McKenzie & Holland frame. The box replaced an earlier cabin in 1905 and remained in use until 25th November 2001. (R.S. Carpenter Photos)

46. Remaining more or less in the same position, the photographer turned in the opposite direction and recorded an N7 arriving with a Palace Gates - North Woolwich train. Comparison with photo No. 40 reveals that the wooden buildings had been subject to alterations since pre-grouping times. Behind the wooden fence to the right we can see the canopies of the Enfield line platforms. (R.S. Carpenter Photos)

47. We take our leave of the branch platforms with this view, looking towards the junction from the up platform shortly before the Palace Gates service was withdrawn. The wooden structures lingered on for a while after closure, but were eventually demolished in the second half of the 1960s. (The Lens of Sutton Collection)

48. Returning to the Enfield line platforms, we stand on the down side and look north some time around 1963. Just beyond the running-in board on the left we see the stairway which provided access to and from the branch, although the attendant post-nationalisation white-on-blue vitreous enamel sign which previously read *"To Palace Gates Platform 4"* has had its lettering painted out. (The Lens of Sutton Collection)

49. Moving over to the up side, we continue looking north, but gain a much closer look at the platform buildings, as they appeared in the late 1960s. They seem to have changed very little since the previous view was taken although fluorescent lighting has replaced the earlier lamps. (I. Baker)

50. Following the opening of the Victoria Line tube station at Seven Sisters, arrangements were made to provide a better interchange. The original GER street level building in West Green Road closed from 1st December 1968 and a new entrance, utilising a section of the disused Birstall Road subway, was constructed in Seven Sisters Road to serve both routes. The old building and the stairways which served the earlier entrance were subsequently demolished and signs of this work can be seen to the left of this view dating from 1980. The covered access to one of the new stairways is visible in the middle distance. (J.E. Connor)

51. On the same day, an EMU is seen entering the station whilst working between Enfield Town and Liverpool Street. By this time the days of the old platform buildings were numbered and demolition followed soon after. (J.E. Connor)

52. All signs of the Great Eastern buildings have now been eradicated as is apparent from this view which shows unit No. 315 854 calling at the down platform in February 2004. (J.E. Connor)

53. On the same day we see the entrance in Seven Sisters Road which serves both Underground and ex-GER stations. It is located at the south end of the station whereas its predecessor, in West Green Road, stood at the north. (J.E. Connor)

BRUCE GROVE

Bruce Grove station, which opened on 22nd July 1872 is located 6 miles 31 chains from Liverpool Street and can be seen near the top of this Ordnance Survey map of 1894.

54. We start our look at the station with this view taken in the early twentieth century after the introduction of electric tramcars. The photographer was standing in the High Road and record-ed a corner of the street level building on the left, together with the bridge carrying the tracks over Bruce Grove itself. This bridge must have been fairly new at the time, as it was reported as having to be lengthened in the GER Ways & Works Committee minutes of 16th February 1904, to facilitate road widening. It seems odd to think that electric street lamps such as that seen in the left foreground were once regarded by some as being unpleasantly modern. In 1888, a contributor to the '*St. James's Gazette*' showed his contempt for new technology when he wrote: "*Twinkle, twinkle little arc. Sickly blue uncertain spark; Up above my head you swing, Ugly, strange expensive thing!*" (Commercial postcard / P. Laming Collection)

Down.	mrn	mrn	mrn	mrn	mrn	mrn	mrn	mrn	mrn	mrn	mrn	mrn	mrn	aft	aft	aft	aft	aft	aft	aft	aft	aft	aft	aft	aft	aft
L'poolSt.d	10 9	1012	1025	1033	1040	1057	11 3	1114	1125	1132	1142	1156	12 2	1210	1225	1232	1240	1255	1 2	1 10	1 18	1 21	1 25	1 32	1 40	1 46
Bishpsgte	1011	1014	1027	1035	1042	1059	11 5	1116	1127	1134	1144	1158	12 4	1212	1227	1234	1242	1257	1 4	1 12	1 20	1 23	1 27	1 34	1 42	1 48
BethnlGrn	1014	1017	1030	1038	1045	11 5	11 8	1119	1130	1137	1147	12 1	12 7	1215	1230	1237	1245	1 6	1 7	1 15	....	1 26	1 30	1 37	1 45	1 51
Cambdg H.	1017	1020	1033	1041	1048	11 8	1111	1122	1133	1140	1150	12 4	1210	1218	1233	1240	1248	1 8	1 10	1 18	....	1 28	1 33	1 40	1 48	1 53
Londn Fld	1019	1022	1035	1043	1050	1110	1113	1124	1135	1142	1152	12 6	1212	1220	1235	1242	1250	1 5	1 12	1 20	....	1 30	1 35	1 42	1 50	1 55
HcknyDns	1021	1025	1038	1046	1053	1113	1116	1127	1138	1145	1155	12 9	1215	1223	1238	1245	1253	1 8	1 15	1 23	1 27	1 33	1 38	1 45	1 53	1 58
Claptn [St	1025	....	1049	....	1119	....	1148	....	1218	....	1248	....	1 18	....		1 36	....	1 43	....	2 1						
St. Jams's	1029	....	1053	....	1123	....	1152	....	1222	....	1252	....	1 22	Satrdys only	1 40	....	1 52	....	2 5							
Hoe St.	1031	....	1055	....	1125	....	1154	....	1224	....	1254	....	1 24	....	1 42	....	1 54	....	2 7							
Wood St.	1034	....	1059	....	1128	....	1157	....	1227	....	1257	....	1 27	....	1 45	....	1 57	....	2 10							
Hale End	1039	....	11 4	....	1133	....		....	1232	....	Sat.	....	1 32	....		....	2	....								
Chingfrd	1043	....	11 8	....	1137	....		....	1236	....	Sat.	....	1 36	....		....	2 6	....								
Rectory Road	1028	1041	....	1056	1116	....	1130	1141	....	1158	1212	....	1226	1241	....	1256	1 11	....	1 26	1 30	1 41	....	1 56			
Stoke Newngtn	1030	1043	....	1058	1118	....	1132	1143	....	12 0	1214	....	1228	1243	....	1258	1 13	....	1 28	1 32	1 43	....	1 58			
Stamford Hill	1033	1046	....	11 1	1121	....	1135	1146	....	12 3	1217	....	1231	1246	....	1 1	1 16	....	1 31	1 35	1 46	....	2 1			
Seven Sisters	1036	1049	....	11 4	1124	....	1138	1149	....	12 6	1220	....	1234	1249	....	1 4	1 19	....	1 34	1 38	1 49	....	2 4			
West Green	....	....	....	11 6	....	....	1140	....	....	12 8	....	....	1236	....	....	1 6	....	....	1 36	....	....	....	2 6			
Green Lanes	....	....	....	1110	....	....	1144	....	....	1212	....	....	1240	....	....	1 10	....	....	1 40	....	....	....	2 10			
Palace Gates	....	....	....	1113	....	....	1146	....	....	1214	....	....	1242	....	....	1 12	....	....	1 42	....	....	....	2 12			
Bruce Grove	1038	1051	....	1126	....	....	1151	....	....	1222	....	....	1251	....	....	1 21	....	....	1 40	1 51	....	....				
White Hart Ln	1041	1054	....	1129	....	....	1154	....	....	1225	....	....	1254	....	....	1 24	....	....	1 43	1 54	....	....				
Silver Street	1044	1057	....	1132	....	....	1157	....	....	1228	....	....	1257	....	....	1 27	....	....	1 46	1 57	....	....				
Lwr Edmonton	1047	11 0	....	1135	....	....		....	....	1231	....	....	1 0	....	....	1 30	....	....	1 49	2 0	....	....				
Bush Hill Park	1050	11 3	....	1138	....	....	12 3	....	....	1234	....	....	1 3	....	....	1 33	....	....	1 52	2 3	....	....				
Enfield Town a	1053	11 6	....	1141	....	....	12 6	....	....	1237	....	....	1 6	....	....	1 36	....	....	1 55	2 6	....	....				

February 1890

55. Moving to the opposite side of the bridge, we look in a south-easterly direction towards the station around 1910. The brick structure towering above the parapet is the signal box which was built in a style to harmonise with the platform buildings and was located at the country end of the up side. The box, which dated from 1872, accommodated eleven levers within its McKenzie & Holland frame and remained in use until 2nd September 1934. The GER Ways & Works Committee minutes of 2nd October 1913 include reference to "temporary and perma-nent" refreshment rooms at the station, but give no indication as to where these were situated. (Commercial postcard / P. Laming Collection)

Down.	aft	aft	aft	aft	aft	aft	aft	aft	aft	aft	aft	aft	aft	aft	aft	aft	aft	aft	aft	aft	aft	aft	aft	aft	aft	aft	aft
L'pool St. d	2 2	1 55	2 10	2 16	2 21		2 25	2 32	2 41	2 49	2 55	2 55	3 3	3 10	3 18	3 28	3 32	3 43	3 47	3 55	4 2	4 14	4 25	4 35	4 45	4 56	5 2
Bishpsgte	2 4	1 57	2 12	2 18			2 27	2 34	2 43	2 51		2 57	3 5	3 12	3 20	3 30	3 34	3 45	3 49	3 57	4 4	4 16	4 27	4 37	4 47	4 50	4 58	5 4
Bethnl Grn	2 7	2 0	2 15	2 21			2 30	2 38	2 46	2 56		3	0 3	3 8	3 15	3 23	3 33	3 37	3 48	3 52	4 0	4 7	4 19	4 30	4 40		4 53	5 1	5 7
Cambdg H.	2 10	2 3	2 18	2 23			2 33	2 40	2 49	2 59	3 2	3 3	3 11	3 18	3 26	3 36	3 40	3 51	3 55	4 3	4 10	4 22	4 33	4 43		4 56	5 4	5 10
Londn Flds	2 12	2 5	2 20	2 25			2 35	2 42	2 51	3 1	3 4	3 5	3 13	3 20	3 28	3 38	3 42	3 53	3 57	4 5	4 12	4 24	4 35	4 45		4 58	5 6	5 12
Hckny Dus	2 15	2 8	2 23	2 28	2 31		2 38	2 45	2 54	3 4	3 7	3 8	3 16	3 23	3 31	3 41	3 45	3 56	4 0	4 8	4 15	4 27	4 38	4 48	4 54	5	9 5 15
Claptn [St	2 18			2 31			2 48		3 7		3 19		3 41		3 48		4 3		4 18			4 51					5 18
St. James's	2 22			2 35			2 52		3 11		3 23		3 45		3 52		4 7		4 22			4 55					5 22
Hoe St.	2 24			2 37			2 54		3 13		3 25		3 47		3 54		4 9		4 24			4 57					5 24
Wood St.	2 27			2 40			2 57		3 16		3 28		3 50		3 57		4 12		4 27			5 0					5 27
Hale End	2 32						3 2				3 33				4 2				4 32			5 5					5 32
Chngfrda	2 36						3 6				3 37				4 6				4 36			5 9					5 36
Rectory Road	2 11	2 26		2 34	2 41		2 57		3 10	3 11		3 26	3 34	3 44		3 59		4 11		4 30	4 41			5	4 5 12		
Stoke Newngtn	2 13	2 28		2 36	2 43		2 59		3 12	3 13		3 28	3 36	3 46		4 1		4 13		4 32	4 43			5	7 5 14		
Stamford Hill	2 16	2 31		2 39	2 46		3 2		3 15	3 16		3 31	3 39	3 49		4 4		4 16		4 35	4 46			5	10 5 17		
Seven Sisters	2 19	2 34		2 42	2 49		3 5		3 18	3 19		3 34	3 42	3 52		4 7		4 19		4 38	4 49		5 0	5 13 5 20			
West Green		2 36					3 7					3 36				4 9				4 40			5 15				
Green Lanes		2 40					3 11					3 40				4 13				4 44			5 19				
Palace Gates		2 42					3 13					3 42				4 15				4 46			5 21				
Bruce Grove	2 21			2 44	2 51			3 20	3 21			3 44	3 54				4 21			4 51		5 2		5 22			
White Hart Ln	2 24			2 47	2 54			3 23	3 24			3 47	3 57				4 24			4 54		5 5		5 25			
Silver Street	2 27			2 50	2 57			3 26	3 27			3 50	4 0				4 27			4 57		5 7		5 28			
Lwr Edmonton	2 30			2 53	3 0			3 29	3 30			3 53	4 3				4 30			5 0		5 10		5 31			
Bush Hill Park	2 33			2 56	3 3			3 32	3 33			3 56	4 6				4 33			5 3		5 13		5 34			
Enfield Town	2 36			2 59	3 6			3 35	3 36			3 59	4 9				4 36			5 6		5 16		5 37			

* St. James's Street. † Green Lanes and Noel Park. ‡ Wood Green. § Station for Upper Edmonton.

February 1890

56. Class N7/3 0-6-2T No. 69712 steams into Bruce Grove with a train for Enfield Town in the late 1950s. Apart from the loss of its signal box the station remained substantially little altered for many years, although the southern end of its platforms had been extended to accommodate longer trains in 1905-6. (T. Wright)

57. Standing on the down side looking north around 1960, we can see that pre-electrification work was almost complete and new lamp standards had been erected behind those they were about to replace. (The Lens of Sutton Collection)

58. Here we view the frontage of the street level building from the High Road in the 1970s, before its venerable white-on-blue nameboards had been removed. A new ticket hall was provided around 1979, but the building's external features were largely retained. (J.E. Connor)

59. The 1979 rebuilding was less merciful up above however, as can be seen from this view taken from the up platform in July 1984. The down side buildings had gone completely and had been replaced with a small brick waiting shelter alongside where the stairs surfaced. The rear wall had been reduced in height and, although not apparent from this angle, the roofing over both stairways had been removed. (The South Chingford Railway Circle)

60. An unusual and pleasing alteration was subsequently made at the station when a replacement awning, matching the original, was erected on the down side. This view was taken in February 2004 and shows unit No. 315 854 heading north towards Enfield Town. (J.E. Connor)

ENFIELD TOWN, PALACE GATES, CHINGFORD, WALTHAMSTOW AND LIVERPOOL STREET.

MONDAYS TO SATURDAYS INCLUSIVE.

		a.m	a.m	a.m	a.m	a.m	a.m	a.m		a.m	a.m	a.m	a.m	a.m	a.m	a.m	a.m	a.m	a.m	a.m	a.m	a.m	a.m	a.m	a.m	a.m	a.m	a.m
ENFIELD TOWN	dep.	..	..	..	3 56	..	..	4 47		..	5 16	..	5 36	5 48	..	..	..	6 8	..	6 26	..	6 29	..	6 33	..	..	6 43	
Bush Hill Park	"	..	..	..	3 59	..	..	4 50		..	5 19	..	5 39	5 51	..	..	..	6 11	..	..	..	6 32	..	6 36	..	..	..	
Lower Edmonton	"	..	..	..	4 3	..	..	4 54		..	5 23	..	5 43	5 55	..	..	..	6 16	..	6 32	..	..	..	6 40	..	..	6 48	
Silver Street	"	..	..	..	4 5	..	..	4 56		..	5 25	..	5 45	5 57	..	..	..	6 18	..	..	..	6 37	..	6 43	..	..	..	
White Hart Lane	"	..	..	..	4 8	..	..	4 59		..	5 28	..	5 48	6 0	..	..	..	6 21	..	6 36	..	..	..	6 45	..	..	6 52	
Bruce Grove	"	..	..	..	4 11	..	..	5 2		..	5 31	..	5 51	6 3	..	..	..	6 24	..	..	..	6 41	..	6 48	..	..	..	
Seven Sisters	arr.	..	..	..	4 13	..	..	5 4		..	5 33	..	5 53	6 5	..	..	..	6 26	..	6 39	..	..	..	6 51	..	..	6 56	
PALACE GATES	dep.	..	..	..	..	..	..	..		5 21	..	..	..	..	..	..	6 2	..	6 26	..	..	..	..	..	6 46	..	
Noel Park & Wood Green	"	..	..	..	..	..	..	..		5 23	..	..	..	..	..	..	6 4	..	6 28	..	..	..	..	..	6 48	..	
West Green	"	..	..	..	..	..	..	..		5 26	..	..	..	..	..	..	6 7	..	6 31	..	..	..	..	..	6 51	..	
Seven Sisters	arr.	..	..	..	..	..	..	..		5 28	..	..	..	..	..	..	6 9	..	6 33	..	..	..	..	..	6 53	..	
Seven Sisters	dep.	..	..	..	4 14	..	..	5 5		..	5 34	..	5 54	6 6	..	..	..	6 27	..	6 40	..	..	..	6 51	..	..	6 57	
Stamford Hill	"	..	..	..	4 17	..	..	5 8		..	5 37	..	5 57	6 9	..	..	..	6 30	..	..	..	6 45	..	6 54	..	..	..	
Stoke Newington	"	..	..	..	4 20	..	..	5 11		..	5 40	..	6 0	6 12	..	..	..	6 33	..	6 45	..	..	..	6 57	..	..	7 2	
Rectory Road	"	..	..	..	4 22	..	..	5 13		..	5 42	..	6 2	6 14	..	..	..	6 35	..	..	..	..	..	6 59	..	..	..	
CHINGFORD	dep.	12 55	..	..	..	4 47	..	..		5 13	..	5 40	..	..	6 0	..	6 12	..	..	..	6 31	..	6 37	..	..	..	
Highams Park	"	12 59	..	..	..	4 52	..	..		5 18	..	5 45	..	..	6 5	..	6 17	..	..	..	6 41	..	6 41	..	..	..	
Wood Street	"	1 2	4 3	4 4	..	4 31	4 56	..		5 22	..	5 49	..	..	6 9	..	6 21	..	6 32	..	..	..	6 45	..	6 53	..	
Hoe Street	"	1 7	3 7	3 7	4 7	4 34	4 59	..		5 25	..	5 52	..	..	6 12	..	6 24	..	6 35	..	..	..	6 49	..	6 56	..	
St. James' St.	"	1 9	3 9	3 9	4 9	4 36	5 2	..		5 28	..	5 55	..	..	6 15	..	6 27	..	..	..	6 46	..	6 51	..	..	..	
Clapton	"	1 13	2 13	3 13	4 13	4 40	5 5	..		5 32	..	5 59	..	..	6 19	..	6 31	..	6 40	..	6 50	..	6 55	..	..	..	
Hackney Downs	"	1 16	2 16	3 16	4 16	4 25	4 44	5 10	5 16	5 36	..	5 45	6 3	6 23	..	6 35	6 38	6 44	..	6 50	..	5 54	6 56	7 2	7 6	..	7 6
London Fields	"	1 18	2 18	3 18	4 18	4 28	..	5 19	..	5 48	..	6 0	8 6	6 20	..	..	..	6 41	..	..	..	..	..	..	..	..	..	
Cambridge Heath	"	1 21	2 21	3 21	4 21	4 31	..	5 22	..	5 51	..	6 11	6 23	..	..	..	6 44	..	6 54	..	7 4	..	..	..	..	7 10	
Bethnal Green	"	1 24	2 24	3 24	4 24	4 33	4 49	5 15	5 24	5 41	..	5 53	6 8	6 14	6 25	6 28	..	6 40	6 46	6 49	..	6 56	..	7 4	7 11	..	7 13
LIVERPOOL ST.	arr.	1 27	2 27	3 27	4 27	4 37	4 53	5 19	5 28	5 45	..	5 57	6 12	6 17	6 29	6 32	..	6 44	6 50	6 53	..	7 0	7 2	7 7	8 7	12 7	7 14

Unless otherwise shown, passengers from **Palace Gates, Noel Park** and **West Green** change at Seven Sisters.

1930

WHITE HART LANE

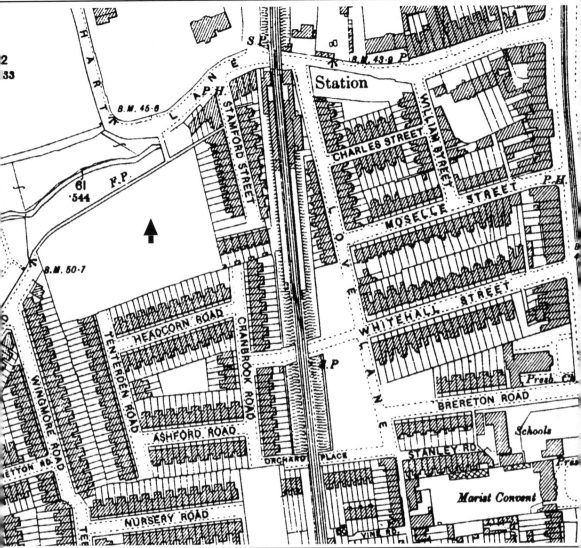

White Hart Lane, located 7 miles 13 chains from Liverpool Street opened on 22nd July 1872 and was constructed in a similar style to the other stations on the line brought into use on the same date. It was provided with a brick signal box at the northern end of its down platform and, when inspected on 27th August 1873, this accommodated twelve levers within a McKenzie & Holland frame. In common with other stations on the GER Enfield route, White Hart Lane retained its original fabric for many years, although, according to the GER Ways & Works Committee minutes, *"improvements"* took place towards the end of 1892, although further details were seemingly not recorded. Authorisation was given to extend the platforms southwards on 21st November 1905 and, a few years later, on 20th June 1912, the Committee agreed to provide an additional exit for the use of soccer fans visiting the nearby football ground. In 1921, the number of levers within the signal box was increased to twenty, but it seems that no further changes took place before the cabin closed on 2nd September 1934 as part of the scheme to install colour-light signalling. The station can be seen towards the top of this Ordnance Survey map of 1894.

61. Here we see a group of staff posing in front a running-in board. The actual date is unknown, but the photograph was probably taken in the first decade of the twentieth century. (Harwich Railway & Shipping Museum)

62. Class N7/4 0-6-2T No. 69621 is seen arriving at the up platform with a Liverpool Street - Enfield working in the late 1950s. The train was presumably running "wrong line" due to engineering works connected with the electrification project. (T. Wright)

63. Three light engines, with an ex-GER 0-6-0 in the foreground, are seen on the up line at White Hart Lane, possibly on the same day that the previous photograph was taken. (T. Wright)

64. A general view of White Hart Lane, looking north around the time of electrification, with new platform lighting in place ready to replace the earlier lamps. The new lights displayed the station's name on their shades, so the earlier totem signs were made redundant and removed. One of the totems can be seen on the left, twisted round to face the photographer, whilst at the end of the platform, what appears to be the lower part of the former signal box can just be glimpsed beyond the canopy. A further entrance / exit for soccer fans was added in 1962. (The Lens of Sutton Collection)

65. By the 1970s when this view was taken, the station was beginning to look rather run-down. It received serious fire damage around 1977, but was subsequently repaired. (I. Baker)

66. A new street level building was subsequently erected on the up side along with steel staircases to serve both platforms. Here we see the station entrance as it appeared in February 2004. (J.E. Connor)

67. The renovation work resulted in the roofing being removed from the stairways, but modified GER-style awnings can still be seen on both platforms, with that on the down side being much shorter than the up. We end our visit to the station with this view taken in February 2004, which shows unit No. 315 860 arriving on a service for Liverpool Street. As can be seen, newer lamps have now replaced those which were erected around the time of electrification. (J.E. Connor)

WHITE HART LANE GOODS

The goods depot at White Hart Lane was located north of the passenger station and opened in the same year. On 11th September 1872 the GER Directors were informed that the sidings were to be inspected by the Board of Trade and fourteen days later it was announced that the Inspecting Officer approved of them being brought into use.

The depot was subsequently enlarged over the years, with coal offices being added in 1883. It was obviously deemed useful as in December 1899 two additional sidings were approved to relieve overcrowding at the big Temple Mills yard near Stratford.

The depot eventually succumbed to road competition and closed from 2nd July 1977. It can be seen on this Ordnance Survey map of 1894, alongside the passenger lines.

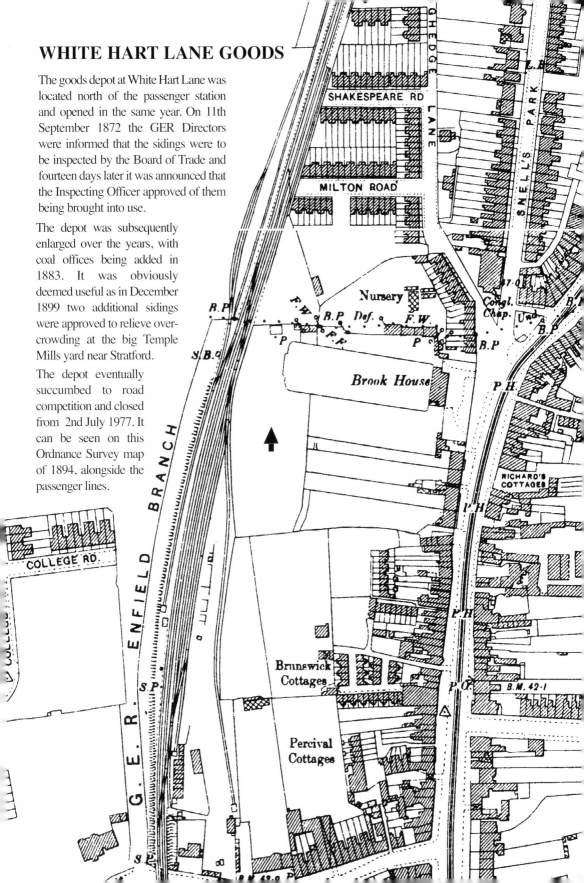

SILVER STREET

Often shown as Silver Street (Upper Edmonton) from the pre-grouping era until BR days, the station opened on 22nd July 1872. It is located 7 miles 75 chains from Liverpool Street and can be seen near the centre of this Ordnance Survey map of 1894.

Silver Street Station

68. This general view, looking southwards in the early 1960s shows the station as it appeared soon after electrification. New platform lighting has replaced the old, but the decapitated remains of the earlier lamp posts remain in-situ. The signal box, which accomodated ten levers within a McKenzie & Holland frame served its intended purpose from 1872 until 2nd September 1934 and was located at the London end of the down platform. (The Lens of Sutton Collection)

69. Walking towards the exit, the photographer pointed his camera in the opposite direction and took this view looking towards Enfield Town. The station was little altered over the years, with the only major change being the lengthening of platforms authorised in November 1905. In addition, the lower sections of the distinctive saw-tooth canopy valances were cropped at some time, but the date when this was done could not be traced. (The Lens of Sutton Collection)

70. By the early 1970s the down platform buildings had been removed, but those on the opposite side remained. This view looks south and includes what is assumed to be the former signal box on the right. (Photographer unknown)

71. By 1973, when this view was taken, the old box had been demolished, but the up side buildings and awning continued to stand. (I. Baker)

72. Moving to the opposite end of the station, we take a further look at the up side buildings in 1973. (I. Baker)

73. Here we see the street level building in September 1982 with stairs ascending to the up platform on the right. The station was badly damaged by fire on 12th June 1984 and much of the remaining GER fabric was subsequently demolished. (The South Chingford Railway Circle)

74. The old street level building was removed after the fire and replaced by a new entrance during 1985-6. This view shows the structure as it appeared in February 2004. (J.E. Connor)

75. Up above the premises had also been largely rebuilt, although a short section of GER awning was retained on the up side. The roofed structure adjoining this is a recent addition, but the little brick shelter serving the down platform is thought to date from the 1970s. The photograph was taken from the south end of the station in February 2004 and looks towards Enfield Town. (J.E. Connor)

EDMONTON GREEN

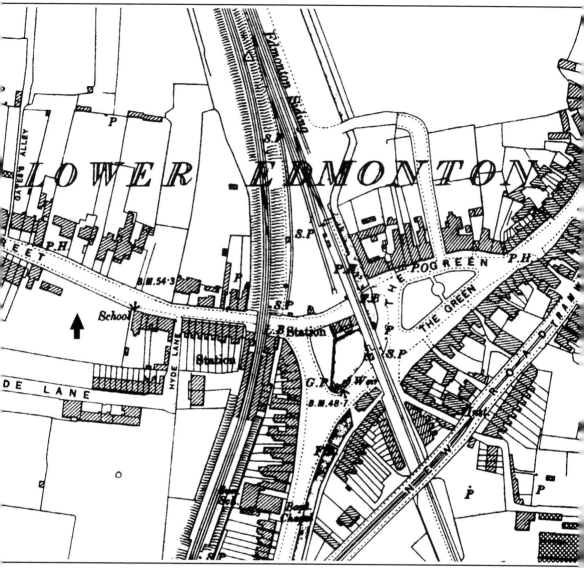

Opened on 22nd July 1872 as 'Edmonton', the station was located 8miles 48chains from Liverpool Street and was renamed Lower Edmonton on 1st July 1883. The brick-built signal box was located at the country end of the up side and accommodated twenty levers within a McKenzie & Holland frame. This dated from the time of opening and remained in use until 2nd September 1934, when it was abolished in connection with the colour light signalling scheme. The station can be seen near the bottom of this Ordnance Survey map of 1894 on the line to the left. The other formation shown joining from the right is the original route from Angel Road which opened in 1849 and included a single platform station subsequently known as Lower Edmonton Low Level. This was latterly only used by workmen's trains and closed to regular passenger traffic from 11th September 1939. When the route from Hackney Downs was being electrified however, the old station was reopened at certain weekends to serve Enfield services which were being diverted by way of the Lea Valley Line, but this was only a temporary measure and the station returned to being closed after the work was completed.

76. Class N7/5 0-6-2T No. 69668 draws to a stand at Lower Edmonton with a train for Enfield Town in the late 1950s. Authorisation to lengthen the southern ends of the platforms was given in November 1905, but otherwise, apart from the installation of electric lighting and subsequent fitting with BR 'totem' style lamp-tablets, the general appearance of the station changed little since opening. (T. Wright)

77. Moving over to the down platform a year or so later, we see an N7 arriving at the up side with a train for Liverpool Street. By this time the overhead wiring had been erected and fluorescent lighting was in the process of replacing the earlier lamps. (The Lens of Sutton Collection)

78. From the opposite end of the down platform we look north and observe a further N7 hauled train arriving from Enfield Town. The view was probably taken on the same day as photograph No. 77 and shows that the installation of new lighting was still incomplete beyond the limits of the station awnings. (The Lens of Sutton Collection)

79. By 1968 when this photograph was taken, the electric services had become well-established, although the station itself continued to remain little changed. Standing on the up platform, we see unit No. 413, still in the earlier green livery, working a service to Liverpool Street. (I. Baker)

80. A replacement street level building was subsequently erected and the station was renamed Edmonton Green on 28th September 1992. This view looks towards the entrance in 1993 and shows that although this was completely new, the remainder of the premises had otherwise undergone very little in the way of alteration. (I. Baker)

81. We take our leave of the station with this view taken from the down side in February 2004, looking north towards Enfield Town. (J.E. Connor)

EDMONTON JUNCTION

82. Edmonton Junction, located to the north of today's Edmonton Green station, is where the 1872 Hackney Downs line joined the original 1849 route from Angel Road. Here we look north from a footbridge added in the early 1900s and view the signal box which had twenty-five levers within a Saxby & Farmer frame. (Norfolk Railway Society)

83. Looking in the opposite direction we see the original line with its adjoining goods yard to the left and the Hackney Downs route on the right. According to the GER Ways & Works Committee minutes, the footbridge from which the photograph was taken, was provided *"for children"*, presumably attending a nearby school, and it was erected by Shewell & Co. of Hunstanton. (Norfolk Railway Society)

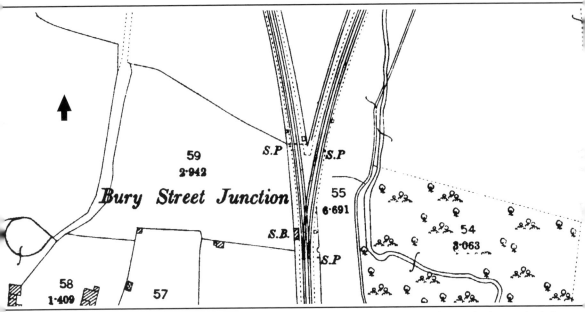

The Ornance Survey map of 1894 shows the junction with the line to Enfield continuing to the left and what is now known as the Southbury Loop diverging towards Cheshunt on the right. As can be seen, the surrounding area remained undeveloped at the time.

84. Standing alongside the down Southbury Loop track in the early 1960s, we look south towards the junction and see the brick base of the former signal box on the right. This box closed on 2nd September 1934 when it was replaced by a ground frame which in turn functioned until 29th May 1960. Consideration was given to the construction of a station at Bury Street, but this failed to materialise. (Norfolk Railway Society)

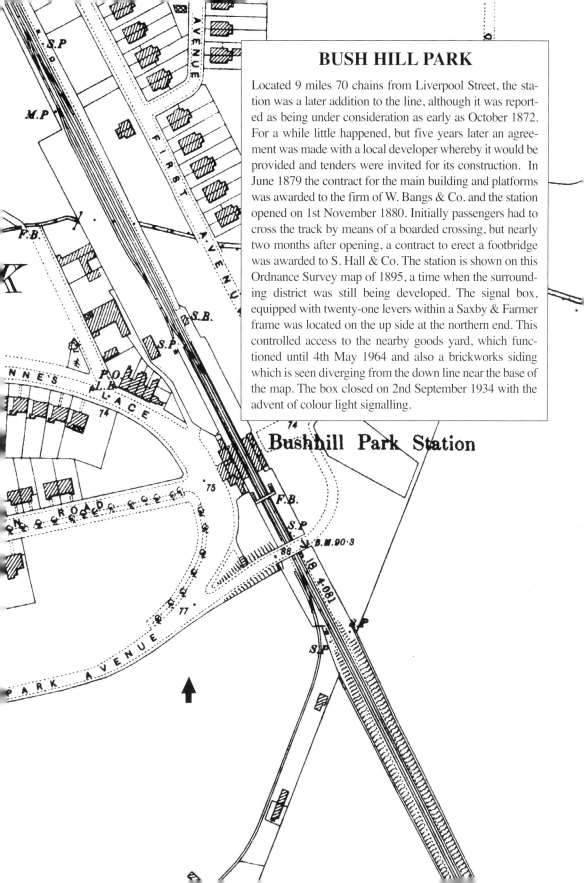

BUSH HILL PARK

Located 9 miles 70 chains from Liverpool Street, the station was a later addition to the line, although it was reported as being under consideration as early as October 1872. For a while little happened, but five years later an agreement was made with a local developer whereby it would be provided and tenders were invited for its construction. In June 1879 the contract for the main building and platforms was awarded to the firm of W. Bangs & Co. and the station opened on 1st November 1880. Initially passengers had to cross the track by means of a boarded crossing, but nearly two months after opening, a contract to erect a footbridge was awarded to S. Hall & Co. The station is shown on this Ordnance Survey map of 1895, a time when the surrounding district was still being developed. The signal box, equipped with twenty-one levers within a Saxby & Farmer frame was located on the up side at the northern end. This controlled access to the nearby goods yard, which functioned until 4th May 1964 and also a brickworks siding which is seen diverging from the down line near the base of the map. The box closed on 2nd September 1934 with the advent of colour light signalling.

Bushhill Park Station

85. This is the main station building, which was located on the down side and was nicely placed to serve the Bush Hill Park villa colony. A decade or so after opening, rows of terraced housing began to be built to the east of the line and an additional booking office was subsequently provided on the opposite platform to serve them. (Commercial postcard / P. Laming Collection)

86. Here we have a nice if somewhat faded view of the station in pre-grouping days, looking south from the down platform towards central London. Plans for the up side booking office were initially aired in 1893 and a contract for its construction was subsequently awarded to the firm of A. Fairhead in July the following year. After this, very few alterations took place for many years, although authority to extend the platforms was given in November 1905. (Commercial postcard / P. Laming Collection)

87. From the northern end of the up platform we look south and see a train for Enfield Town arriving behind a Class N7 0-6-2T at an unknown date, possibly in the 1930s. (Stations UK)

88. This view is again undated, but it was probably taken in the 1950s, when preparatory work on the electrification project was under way. The footbridge has been raised on concrete bases, presumably to clear the overhead wires, but a start was yet to be made on erecting the catenary. A siding for goods traffic is just visible in the distance beyond the end of the down platform. (RAS Marketing)

89. With the end of steam imminent Class N7/5 0-6-2T No.69664 pauses at the up platform with a train for Liverpool Street. (T. Wright)

90. This view looks north towards Enfield Town and shows the up side building erected around 1894, as it appeared in the late 1960s. (I. Baker)

91. The entrance leading to the up platform was a much plainer affair than that built to serve the villa colony on the opposite side of the line. Here it is seen in 1973, before the white-on-blue enamel nameboard was replaced by one of the British Rail corporate image style introduced in the previous decade. (J.E. Connor)

92. The original down side building was severely damaged by fire in August 1981 and replaced the following year by the entrance which is seen here. (J.E. Connor)

93. The 1890s building on the up side remained standing however and is visible in this view taken in February 2004, as a 4-car Class 315 EMU departed for Liverpool Street. (J.E. Connor).

94. Located 10 miles 25 chains from Liverpool Street, Lincoln Road level crossing lays to the south of Enfield Town station. In this view, a young boy stands by the gates and watches a train formed of Class 315 stock hurry past on 14th August 1993. (I. Baker)

95. On the same day we see unit No. 315857 approaching the crossing having just departed from Enfield Town. (I. Baker)

Enfield Town Station

Goods Shed

P.O.

GENOTIN ROAD

BURLEIGH ROAD

B.M.105·2

QU

P

P

P

SCHOOL

103

P

P

S.P.

S.P.

S.P.

S.B.

S.P.

S.P.

S.P.

F.P.

Z·00

L O N D O N

1561
10·593

94

88

B.M.90·2

L.B.

97

97

108

108

108

ENFIELD TOWN

The Ordnance Survey map seen here shows the station with its single island platform as it appeared in 1895.

Opened by the Eastern Counties Railway as 'Enfield' on 1st March 1849, it utilised a late 17th century mansion as its main building. The premises were rebuilt in 1858 and again during the 1870s, when the old mansion was finally demolished. The contract for the new buildings was awarded to the firm of Perry & Co. in May 1872 and five months later the decision was taken to add an adjoining house as residential accommodation for the Station Master.

To the left of the station, the map shows an engine shed, complete with turntable, which had its origins in the late 1860s, although it seems that there had been locomotive facilities at the terminus since its earliest days. Late in 1866 however, it was decided to provide better accommodation and a contract for the construction of a new shed was let to Bell & Sons of Saffron Walden towards the end of January 1867. Soon after, a complaint was received from the New River Company who objected to its siting, so work on the project was temporarily suspended. Unfortunately, the GER was finding itself short of money, so the contractors remained unpaid for a while and in October 1867, a temporary shelter was built to accommodate locomotives during the winter months. Work eventually restarted around May of the following year and it seems to have been completed by 1869.

The station itself underwent a few alterations after its 1870s rebuilding, but these were all of a fairly minor nature. The platform surface was asphalted in 1874 and accommodation for guards was added to the buildings twelve years later. In October 1892 the Ways & Works Committee minutes refer to a scheme to *"improve the covered way"*, although gives no further details. There does not seem to have been a covered way as such, so the item is thought to have referred to the platform awning. In February 1893 a contract to *"extend the covered way"* was let to the local Enfield firm of A. Fairhead and the work was presumably carried out soon after.

96. This view from the early twentieth century shows the entrance erected in the 1870s with the Station Master's house to its left. As can be seen the main building was provided with a lantern roof and was set back from the road behind a walled courtyard. (Commercial postcard / P. Laming Collection)

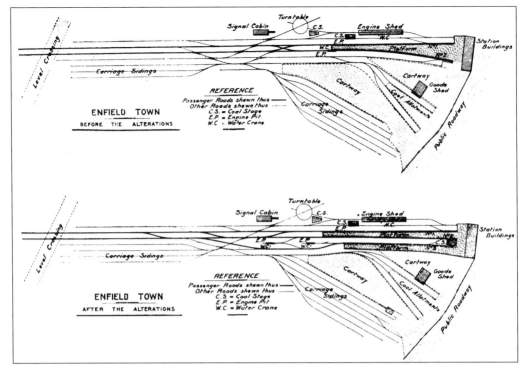

ENFIELD TOWN
BEFORE THE ALTERATIONS

REFERENCE
Passenger Roads shewn thus ——
Other Roads shewn thus - - - -
C.S. = Coal Stage
E.P. = Engine Pit
W.C. = Water Crane

ENFIELD TOWN
AFTER THE ALTERATIONS

REFERENCE
Passenger Roads shewn thus ——
Other Roads shewn thus - - - -
C.S. = Coal Stage
E.P. = Engine Pit
W.C. = Water Crane

These diagrams illustrate the alterations which were carried out at the station in readiness for the 'Jazz Service' of 1920. One of these was the addition of a further platform on the up side, which was brought into use that year. For a brief time it seems that the locomotive turntable was retained but in July 1921 the GER felt that it should be removed as it was *"no longer used"*. (The Railway Gazette)

97. Standing on the island platform in 1931, we look towards the buffer stops and see a train for Liverpool Street about to depart. Part of the engine shed is visible on the left, albeit in deep shadow, whilst the platform added in 1920 appears to the right, with the goods shed in the middle distance. In March 1919 the GER Ways & Works Committee stated that by way of a trial, the station, loco shed and goods depot were to be illuminated with Sugg's inverted gas burners. (H.C. Casserley)

98. Over the years, the entrance building lost the decorative ironwork around the top of its roof and also its walled forecourt. This photograph dates from the 1950s and was probably taken shortly before station modernisation resulted in its demolition. Its replacement, erected during 1957-8, was designed by the British Railways' architect, H.H. Powell. (The Lens of Sutton Collection)

99. With station rebuilding in its early stages, we stand behind the buffer stops in the 1950s and see that the old loco release road which adjoined the engine shed had been removed in order that the island platform could be widened. (K. Fairey)

100. Rebuilding was completed by the Spring of 1958 and included a new 418ft long concrete and glass awning on the island. This view was taken from the north end of Platform 1 in the final days of steam operation and includes the loco shed on the right. (The Lens of Sutton Collection)

101. Moving over to the platform added in 1920 we have a good view of the modernised premises with a Class N7 0-6-2T in the process of running-round her train. The goods yard, which lay to the east of the passenger station closed from 14th September 1959. (The Lens of Sutton Collection)

102. Standing on the island platform, we take a last look at the station in steam days. An N7 hauled train awaits departure for Liverpool Street on the right, whilst a member of the same class is seen on the left standing outside the engine shed. By now the shed's days were numbered, as it closed towards the end of 1960 and was subsequently demolished. (The Lens of Sutton Collection)

103. Moving on to more recent times, we stand in the forecourt and view the station frontage in February 2004. (J.E. Connor)

104. Still in February 2004, we look northwards along the island platform and see passengers alighting from a Class 315 electric unit on the right which has just worked in from Liverpool Street. (J.E. Connor)

105. We take our leave of the Enfield Town line with this view of unit No. 315 845 arriving at the terminus in February 2004. The signal box seen on the right dated from 1905 and was originally equipped with a seventy-eight lever McKenzie & Holland frame. This was replaced by a new twenty-five lever Westinghouse frame in 1959, but the box itself soldiered on until it was abolished on 25th November 2001. (J.E. Connor)

Palace Gates Branch

WEST GREEN

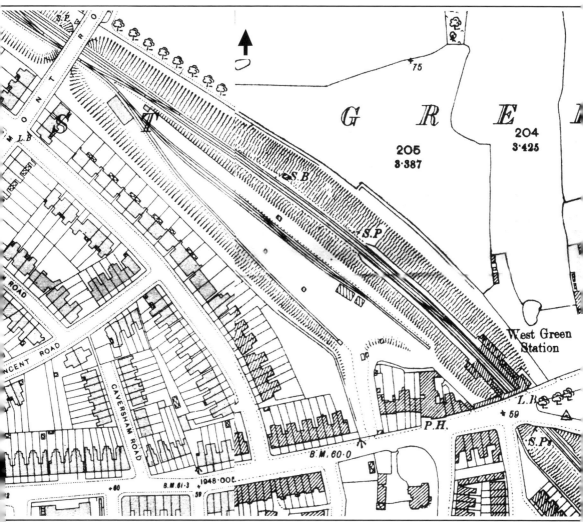

West Green was the first station on the Palace Gates branch and was located 53 chains from Seven Sisters. It comprised two platforms and was entered by way of a street level building on the north side of West Green Road. This Ordnance Survey map of 1894 shows the layout and includes the goods depot which lay on the down side. Both station and depot were brought into use on 1st January 1878, although the latter was subsequently enlarged and around the end of 1880 was provided with a siding specifically for the use of the North London Dairy Company.

Further expansion was authorised on 1st June 1897, when the GER Ways & Works Committee minutes recorded that *"additional goods facilities"* were to be installed. Access to the yard was controlled by a wooden signal box with a twenty-lever McKenzie & Holland frame, which stood to the north-west of the up passenger platform. The station itself seems to have remained little altered for much of its existence, although in November 1905, the company decided to lengthen both platforms so that longer trains could be accommodated.

106. This view looks towards Seven Sisters from the up side some time in the 1930s. The building at street level was constructed of brick, but those on the platform were largely wooden. The style of canopy valancing is that which was favoured by the GER in the late nineteenth and early twentieth centuries, so this may have post-dated the station's opening. (Stations UK)

107. Class F7 2-4-2T No. 8300 brings the Palace Gates - Seven Sisters shuttle into West Green, again in the 1930s. The set comprises three clerestory roofed coaches, which were specially modified for push-pull working and had previously seen service on the Churchbury Loop. In the middle distance, we can catch a glimpse of West Green signal box, which officially remained operational until 7th February 1965. (Photographer unknown / J.E. Connor Collection)

108. The street level building with its rather plain frontage almost certainly dated from the station's opening in 1878. On 31st December 1879, the GER Directors' minutes referred to the addition of *"four coal offices"* which are presumably those which can be seen adjoining the doorway on the left. After closure, the platform buildings were demolished around 1968 but the former entrance lasted a little longer. The four coal offices were noted as still standing in October 2001, but are understood to have been demolished soon after. (The Lens of Sutton Collection)

NOEL PARK GOODS DEPOT

The goods depot lay to the south-east of Noel Park & Wood Green station and can be seen on this Ordnance Survey map of 1912. It opened with the line on 1st January 1878 and was originally referred to as Green Lanes.

In connection with the Wood Green Charter Jubilee celebrations, an exhibition of locomotives and rolling stock was staged here between 12th and 14th September 1958. Special edmondson tickets were produced for the event and all proceeds went to charity. The exhibition was very successful and during its three days was visited by around 14,000 people.

The yard, which was operated from a six-lever Saxby & Farmer ground frame, remained in use until 7th December 1964, although the frame was not officially abolished until 31st January 1965.

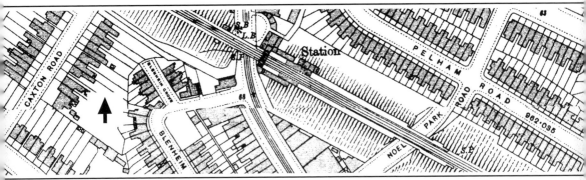

The station, which opened as Green Lanes on 1st January 1878, was located 1 mile 49 chains from Seven Sisters and is shown on this Ordnance Survey map of 1912. During the early 1880s, the Artizans' Labourers' & General Dwellings Company was in the process of erecting its Noel Park housing estate nearby and, in recognition of this, the station was renamed Green Lanes (Noel Park), or Green Lanes & Noel Park as it was sometimes shown, on 1st May 1884. A further change came on 1st January 1902, when it became Noel Park & Wood Green.

109. This early twentieth century view of Wood Green High Road, taken after the introduction of electric tramcars, includes part of the station's down side exit on the right. On 3rd October 1882, the GER Ways & Works Committee agreed to lengthen the platforms, but problems with a bridge abutment resulted in delay. This was duly rectified by underpinning and a contract for the extension was awarded to the firm of J. Oswald Gardener in September 1883. Further problems were experienced in November 1905, when drainage excavations which were being carried out by the local council caused two abutment wing walls to crack. The station served for a while as a temporary branch terminus, and the signal box, seen on the left, dated from that period. It housed a sixteen-lever Saxby & Farmer frame and remained in use until 27th September 1936 when it was abolished in connection with road widening. (Commercial postcard / P. Laming Collection)

Tramway albums from Middleton Press covering the area of this volume include :-
Stamford Hill Tramways   Waltham Cross & Edmonton Tramways
Enfield & Wood Green Tramways

110. Ex-GER Class F7 2-4-2T No 8304 arrives with a two-coach push-pull set in the 1930s, whilst working the Palace Gates - Seven Sisters shuttle service. The station was still largely in its original condition at the time, although approval to add further platform extensions had been given in November 1905. The roof of the signal box is just visible behind the leading carriage. (Pamlin Prints)

111. Plans to rebuild the station were first mooted in May 1937, but financial restraints resulted in the work being delayed. It was eventually carried out around the early part of 1939 however, and resulted in new concrete platforms and replacement waiting shelters. This view looks towards Palace Gates from the up side and was probably taken around 1960. (Stations UK)

112. From the west end of the up platform we see Class N7/3 0-6-2T No. 69723 arriving at the station with a North Woolwich - Palace Gates train in the early 1960s. (T. Wright)

113. The rebuilding scheme of the late 1930s initially envisaged that the street level building would be replaced by one which included both office and shop accommodation. The plan was soon scaled down however and the existing structure was given a partial facelift instead. Here the station is seen from the opposite side of Wood Green High Road. The building was subsequently converted for use as commercial premises around 1969, but within a few years all had gone to provide a site for the Wood Green Shopping City development. (The Lens of Sutton Collection)

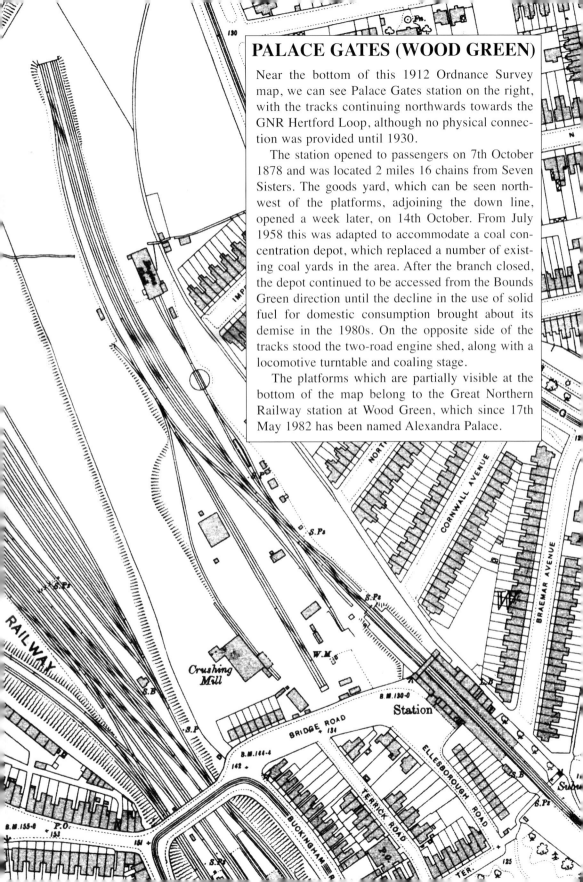

PALACE GATES (WOOD GREEN)

Near the bottom of this 1912 Ordnance Survey map, we can see Palace Gates station on the right, with the tracks continuing northwards towards the GNR Hertford Loop, although no physical connection was provided until 1930.

The station opened to passengers on 7th October 1878 and was located 2 miles 16 chains from Seven Sisters. The goods yard, which can be seen northwest of the platforms, adjoining the down line, opened a week later, on 14th October. From July 1958 this was adapted to accommodate a coal concentration depot, which replaced a number of existing coal yards in the area. After the branch closed, the depot continued to be accessed from the Bounds Green direction until the decline in the use of solid fuel for domestic consumption brought about its demise in the 1980s. On the opposite side of the tracks stood the two-road engine shed, along with a locomotive turntable and coaling stage.

The platforms which are partially visible at the bottom of the map belong to the Great Northern Railway station at Wood Green, which since 17th May 1982 has been named Alexandra Palace.

114. This view looks towards the north end of the station as it appeared around 1910. The tracks leading to the engine shed veer to the left, whilst the goods yard can be seen on the right. The chimney stacks on the station footbridge were necessary because both towers were provided with fireplaces to keep the structure warm in winter. (British Rail)

115. The engine shed possibly dated from the line's opening, although both the building and its associated facilities were subjected to various alterations over the years. In June 1889, the GER Ways & Works Committee recommended additional sidings and a pit for loco servicing, then in 1904, ventilation louvres were added to the roof. The depot continued to function into the first half of the 1950s, but probably closed soon after. Here we see its south end around 1911. (British Rail)